Writing and Storytelling for 21st Century Audiences

By Niket Mehta

Introduction

Welcome to the Wonderful World of Storytelling!

Have you ever been captivated by a movie that left you speechless? Or devoured a book so enthralling you couldn't put it down? The power of storytelling is undeniable. It transports us to different worlds, ignites our imaginations, and connects us on a deep emotional level.

As aspiring creators in the field of animation and multimedia, you hold the keys to unlocking exciting new frontiers in storytelling. This book is your guide on this thrilling journey. We'll delve into the essential elements of crafting compelling narratives, from developing captivating characters to constructing intricate plots and weaving worlds that come alive.

Whether you dream of creating heart-wrenching animated films, interactive games that immerse players in epic adventures, or captivating graphic novels that push the boundaries of the medium, this book will equip you with the tools and techniques you need to bring your stories to life.

But storytelling is more than just technical expertise. It's about understanding what resonates with audiences, exploring the power of emotions, and harnessing the ability to evoke laughter, tears, and everything in between. We'll explore diverse storytelling methods, delve into the ethical considerations of crafting narratives, and learn how to effectively market and pitch your ideas.

This book is not just a collection of information; it's an interactive experience. This book is divided into five modules and at the end of each module of the book a story is given based upon the concepts discussed in that module and illustrates the basic concepts of storytelling introduced in that module. This book provides you with practical exercises to hone your writing skills, encourage you to analyze successful stories, and guide you through the exciting process of developing your own unique voice as a storyteller.

This book is divided into 5 modules and after each module there is an example story which learners can write after learning from respective module. There are review questions and practical exercises after each chapter which would help in revision and practical execution of the knowledge. Teacher can conduct these exercises in a workshop or after their class lectures.

So, grab your digital pen, fire up your animation software, or get your sketchpad ready. It's time to unleash your creativity and embark on a journey to become a master storyteller!

About the Author

Dr. Niket Mehta working as Assistant Professor in Animation and Multimedia Department, Birla Institute of Technology, Mesra, Ranchi, Noida Campus, India since 2005. He has done PhD, MCA, MBA, and MA English and diplomas in Advertising, Advance Computer Arts, Non-Linear Editing etc. He has attended and organized various conferences and Faculty Development Programmes. He has presented papers at various conferences of repute and published papers in journals, proceedings, book chapters etc. He has written 3 monographs. He also takes care of social media and cultural activities. He has made a Science Documentary film on fourth state of matter – Plasma, Interactive animated E-learning Module for army and for University students on Research Methodology and Advertising subjects, designed Print Media and Social Media Advertisement campaigns etc. apart from his many other creative and academic pursuits.

Index

Module 1: Introduction to Storytelling

1. **Understanding Storytelling and Its Importance**

   – Definition and elements of storytelling

   – Importance of storytelling in multimedia and animation

2. **History and Evolution of Storytelling**

   – Oral traditions, myths, and legends

   – Evolution of storytelling through different media

3. **Narrative Structures**

   – Linear vs. non-linear storytelling

   – Three-act structure and other narrative frameworks

4. **Genres and Styles**

   – Overview of different storytelling genres (e.g., fantasy, science fiction, drama)

- Styles of storytelling (e.g., first-person, third-person)

5. **Audience and Purpose**
   - Identifying and understanding target audiences
   - Purpose and message in storytelling

6. **Case Studies**
   - Analysis of successful storytelling in multimedia
   - Discussion of popular stories and their impact

Module 2: Character Development

1. **Creating Memorable Characters**
   - Traits of compelling characters
   - Protagonists, antagonists, and supporting characters

2. **Character Arcs and Growth**
   - Importance of character development over the narrative

- Types of character arcs

3. **Dialogue and Interaction**

   - Writing authentic dialogue

   - Interactions between characters

4. **Character Design in Animation**

   - Visual design principles for animated characters

   - Integrating visual and narrative elements

5. **Case Studies**

   - Analysis of well-developed characters in animation and multimedia

6. **Workshop**

   - Creating and developing characters for a class project

Module 3: Plot and Structure

1. **Plot Development**

   - Elements of a good plot

   - Techniques for plot development

2. **Conflict and Resolution**

    – Types of conflict (internal vs. external)

    – Crafting satisfying resolutions

3. **Pacing and Timing**

    – Importance of pacing in storytelling

    – Techniques to control narrative timing

4. **Subplots and Parallel Storylines**

    – Integrating subplots into the main narrative

    – Managing multiple storylines

5. **Plot Devices and Twists**

    – Common plot devices (e.g., flashbacks, foreshadowing)

    – Crafting effective plot twists

6. **Workshop**

    – Developing and outlining plots for a class project

Module 4: Writing for Multimedia

1. **Writing for Animation**

- Techniques for writing animation scripts
- Differences between writing for animation and live-action

2. **Interactive Storytelling**
   - Principles of interactive narratives
   - Writing for video games and interactive media

3. **Transmedia Storytelling**
   - Creating stories across multiple platforms
   - Challenges and strategies for transmedia narratives

4. **Writing for Digital Media**
   - Writing for web series, short films, and online content
   - Adapting traditional writing techniques for digital formats

5. **Visual Storytelling**
   - Importance of visuals in multimedia storytelling

– Integrating text and visuals seamlessly

6. **Case Studies**

– Analysis of successful multimedia storytelling projects

Module 5: Advanced Techniques and Final Project

1. **Experimental Storytelling**

   – Exploring non-traditional storytelling methods

   – Examples of experimental narratives

2. **Adaptation and Remakes**

   – Techniques for adapting existing stories into new formats

   – Challenges of remakes and reboots

3. **Ethical Considerations in Storytelling**

   – Representation, diversity, and inclusion in narratives

   – Ethical storytelling practices

4. **Marketing and Pitching Stories**

- Techniques for pitching stories to producers and studios
- Marketing strategies for storytelling projects

5. **Feedback and Revision**

- Importance of feedback in the writing process
- Techniques for revising and improving narratives

6. **Final Project Presentation**

- Presentation and critique of final storytelling projects
- Class discussion and feedback

Module I

Introduction to Storytelling

Chapter 1: Understanding Storytelling and Its Importance

Welcome to the world of storytelling! This chapter will lay the foundation for your journey into crafting captivating narratives that will come alive through animation and multimedia.

1.1 What is Storytelling?

Storytelling is the art of weaving a narrative that connects with an audience. It's about creating a journey with characters, emotions, and events that resonate with viewers on a personal level.

Here's an analogy: Imagine a delicious meal. The ingredients (characters, events, setting) are all important, but it's the way they are combined and seasoned (plot, theme) that creates a truly satisfying experience.

Stories are all around us. From the bedtime tales we heard as children to the news reports we watch daily, narratives shape our understanding of the world and evoke a range of emotions.

1.2 Elements of Storytelling

Every great story is built on a foundation of key elements. Let's explore these building blocks:

- **Plot:** This is the sequence of events that unfold in your story. It typically follows a structure with a beginning (introduction), middle (development of conflict), and end (resolution).
- **Characters:** These are the individuals who drive the narrative. They can be human, animal, object, or even abstract concepts. Well-developed characters have personalities, motivations, and goals that the audience can connect with.
- **Setting:** This is the environment where the story takes place. Setting can play a crucial role in shaping the plot and atmosphere of your story. Think about the difference between a story set in a bustling city and one set in a quiet forest.

- **Theme:** This is the underlying message or idea your story explores. It's bigger than just the plot and can be explored through the actions of your characters. Themes can be universal, such as love, loss, or hope.
- **Conflict:** Every good story needs a challenge. Conflict creates tension and motivates the characters to act. Conflict can be internal, where a character struggles with themselves, or external, where they face an obstacle or antagonist.
- **Style:** This is the voice and tone of your storytelling. Is it humorous, dramatic, or suspenseful? Your stylistic choices will help to shape the overall experience for your audience.

Image: Different elements of storytelling.

1.3 Why Storytelling Matters in Animation & Multimedia

Storytelling is the heart and soul of animation and multimedia. It's what brings static images and sounds to life, creating an emotional connection with the audience.

Here's why storytelling is so important:

- **Engages and Captivates:** A compelling story grabs the audience's attention and keeps them wanting more. Animation and multimedia can use visuals, sound, and movement to enhance the story's impact, making it truly immersive.

- **Conveys Ideas Effectively:** Stories are powerful communicators. By using relatable characters and situations, animators and multimedia artists can effectively convey complex ideas, messages, and information in a way that is both informative and entertaining.

- **Evokes Emotion:** Stories have the power to make us laugh, cry, feel angry, or inspired. Animations and multimedia projects that tap into these emotions are more likely to resonate with the audience and leave a lasting impression.

- **Shapes Perception:** Stories can shape our understanding of the world, prompting us to think critically and consider different perspectives. Animators and multimedia artists can use storytelling to address social issues, advocate for change, and promote positive messages.

1.4 Case Study: The Power of Storytelling in Animation

Consider the classic animated film "Spirited Away." This movie uses a fantastical story with relatable characters to explore themes of loss, self-discovery, and the importance of courage. The animation style beautifully complements the narrative, creating a visually stunning and emotionally engaging experience for viewers of all ages.

This example highlights how powerful storytelling can be in animation. It doesn't matter if the story is simple or complex; it's the emotional connection that resonates with the audience that truly matters.

1.5 Review Questions

1. Define storytelling in your own words.

2. What are the key elements of a story?

3. Why is storytelling important in animation and multimedia?

4. Can you think of an example of how storytelling has impacted you through animation or multimedia?

1.6 Suggested Practical Exercises

1. **Brainstorming:** Write down ten story ideas. They can be anything that sparks your imagination!

2. **Character Development:** Choose one of your story ideas and develop a main character. Give your character a name, personality, motivation

Chapter 2: History and Evolution of Storytelling

The art of storytelling is as old as humanity itself. Throughout history, we've shared stories around campfires, in grand theaters, and now, on our digital devices. This chapter will delve into the fascinating journey of storytelling, exploring its origins and evolution through different media.

2.1 Oral Traditions: The Roots of Storytelling

Imagine a time before written language. Stories were passed down through generations through oral traditions. People gathered around fires to hear tales of brave heroes, fearsome monsters, and the creation of the world. These stories weren't just entertainment; they were a way to preserve history, teach moral lessons, and create a sense of community.

Myths and Legends: These are traditional stories, often considered true by a culture, that explain natural phenomena, historical events, or cultural beliefs. Myths like the Greek myth of Pandora's Box or the Chinese legend of the Dragon King explore themes of creation, human nature, and the consequences of our actions.

Image: A group gathered around a campfire listening to a storyteller

2.2 The Rise of Written Storytelling

The invention of writing revolutionized storytelling. Stories that were once only passed down orally could now be recorded and shared with a wider audience. Early forms of writing included pictograms, hieroglyphics, and cuneiform scripts. These early written narratives laid the foundation for the development of literature as we know it today.

Impact of Writing:

- **Preservation:** Written stories could be preserved and passed down through generations without the risk of distortion or loss.
- **Complexity:** Writers could now craft more intricate plots and develop characters in greater detail.
- **Spread of Ideas:** Written stories facilitated the spread of knowledge and ideas across cultures and geographical boundaries.

Examples: The Epic of Gilgamesh, the Egyptian Book of the Dead, and the Indian epics Ramayana and Mahabharata are all examples of early written narratives that continue to captivate readers today.

2.3 Storytelling Through Different Media

The evolution of media has constantly shaped how we tell stories.

- **Printing Press:** The invention of the printing press in the 15th century made books more widely available, leading to a boom in storytelling and literacy.

- **Theater & Performance:** Plays and theatrical performances have been a popular medium for storytelling for centuries. From ancient Greek tragedies to modern Broadway musicals, theater offers a dynamic and immersive experience for audiences.

- **Film & Cinema:** The birth of cinema in the late 19th century revolutionized storytelling. Moving images, sound, and music combined to create a new and powerful way to engage audiences.

- **Radio & Television:** Radio and television became dominant mediums for storytelling in the 20th century. These technologies allowed stories to reach a wider audience than ever before.
- **Digital Media:** The rise of digital media has ushered in a new era of storytelling possibilities. The internet, animation software, and video games have all opened up new avenues for creative expression and audience interaction.

Image: A representation of the evolution of storytelling through different media.

2.4 Case Study: Storytelling Across Media - Aesop's Fables

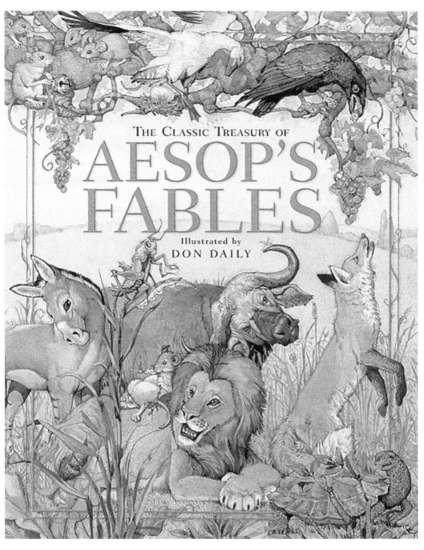

Image Courtesy: Amazon.com

Aesop's Fables, a collection of short stories with moral lessons, offer a fascinating example of storytelling across media. These fables originated as oral traditions and were later written down. Today, they are adapted into animated films, children's books, and even video games. This case study highlights the versatility and enduring power of good storytelling.

2.5 Review Questions

1. How were stories shared before the invention of writing?
2. What are some advantages of written storytelling compared to oral traditions?
3. Discuss the impact of different media (e.g., film, theater, digital media) on storytelling.
4. Can you think of an example of how a story has been adapted across different media platforms?

2.6 Suggested Practical Exercises

1. Choose a traditional story from your culture or another culture and rewrite it as a short script suitable for animation.
2. Research the history of storytelling in a specific region or time period. Create a

presentation or infographic to share your findings.

3. Explore different online storytelling platforms (e.g., interactive fiction, video games). Analyze how these platforms use technology to tell stories in new and engaging ways.

These exercises will help you deepen your understanding of the history and evolution of storytelling and explore its potential in the digital age.

Chapter 3: Narrative Structures

Imagine a delicious meal. You wouldn't just throw all the ingredients together on a plate, would you? A good story, like a good meal, needs a well-defined structure to be truly satisfying. This chapter dives into the world of narrative structures, exploring linear and non-linear storytelling and popular narrative frameworks.

3.1 Linear vs. Non-Linear Storytelling

The most basic distinction in narrative structure is between linear and non-linear storytelling.

- **Linear Storytelling:** This is the classic "beginning, middle, and end" structure. Events unfold in a chronological order, taking the audience on a clear journey with a cause-and-effect relationship. Think of a traditional fairy tale or a superhero movie – these often follow a linear structure.

- **Non-Linear Storytelling:** This type of narrative structure doesn't follow a strict chronological order. Events may jump forward and backward in time, or multiple storylines may be interwoven. Non-linear narratives can be used to create suspense, mystery, or a deeper exploration of character motivations. Films like "Memento" or video games with branching narratives use non-linear storytelling techniques.

Choosing the Right Structure:

The best narrative structure for your story depends on your overall goals.

- **Linear:** A linear structure works well for stories that focus on a clear journey or transformation, making it a good choice for animation aimed at younger audiences.
- **Non-Linear:** Non-linear structures can be more complex and challenging for audiences to follow, but they can also be more rewarding, offering a deeper understanding of the characters and themes.

Linear Story Telling

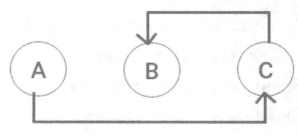

Non Linear Story Telling

Image: A simple diagram contrasting linear and non-linear storytelling

3.2 Example of Linear and Non-Linear Story

Certainly! Let's use a simple story to illustrate both linear and non-linear storytelling.

Linear Story (Chronological Order)

Title: The Lost Necklace

Plot:

1. **Introduction:** Emma is a young girl living in a small village. One day, her grandmother gives her a beautiful, ancient necklace as a gift.

2. **Rising Action:** Emma wears the necklace to a village festival. While playing with her friends, she realizes the necklace is missing.

3. **Climax:** Panicked, Emma retraces her steps, asking everyone if they have seen the necklace. She searches the entire village, but no one has found it.

4. **Falling Action:** After a long day of searching, Emma returns home feeling defeated. As she sits on her bed, she notices something shiny under her pillow—it's the necklace!

5. **Resolution:** Emma learns that her grandmother had secretly taken the necklace back to keep it safe during the festival. She returns it to Emma with a smile, teaching her the value of responsibility.

Non-Linear Story (Mixed Chronology)
Title: The Lost Necklace

Plot:

1. **Scene 1 (Climax):** Emma frantically searches the village, asking everyone if they've seen her lost necklace. She's on the verge of tears, fearing it's gone forever.

2. **Scene 2 (Introduction):** Flashback to the day Emma's grandmother gives her the necklace, explaining its history and significance.

3. **Scene 3 (Rising Action):** Flash forward to Emma wearing the necklace at the village festival, playing with her friends, and then realizing it's missing.

4. **Scene 4 (Falling Action):** Emma returns home, exhausted from the search. She sits on her bed and notices something shiny under her pillow.

5. **Scene 5 (Resolution):** A flashback reveals that Emma's grandmother took the necklace to keep it safe during the festival. The story ends with Emma holding the necklace, understanding the lesson her grandmother intended to teach her.

Analysis:

- Linear Story: Events unfold in a straightforward, chronological sequence, making the story easy to follow and understand.

- Non-Linear Story: The plot jumps back and forth in time, revealing important information out of order. This technique can create suspense, emphasize themes, or provide a deeper understanding of characters and events.

The non-linear approach can make the story more intriguing, as the audience pieces together the timeline, while the linear approach provides a clear and direct narrative.

3.2 The Three-Act Structure: A Storytelling Staple

The three-act structure is a widely used narrative framework, especially in animation and film. It breaks down the story into three distinct parts:

- **Act 1: Set-up (Introduction):** Introduce the characters, setting, and initial conflict of the story. This act establishes the world and stakes for your audience.

- **Act 2: Confrontation (Development):** The main conflict escalates, and the characters face challenges. This is the heart of the story where the action unfolds.

- **Act 3: Resolution (Climax and Ending):** The conflict is resolved, and the story reaches a satisfying conclusion. This act ties up loose ends and leaves a lasting impression on the audience.

While the three-act structure is a valuable tool, it's not a rigid formula. Many stories benefit from variations on this structure. For example, some stories may have a five-act structure, while others might use a circular structure where the ending loops back to the beginning.

3.3 Beyond the Three-Act Structure: Other Narratives Frameworks

There are many other narrative frameworks that can be used to structure a story. Here are a few examples:

- **Hero's Journey:** This mythic structure, popularized by Joseph Campbell, explores the archetypal journey of a hero who leaves their ordinary world, faces challenges, and returns transformed. This framework can be found in countless stories across cultures.

  The Hero's Journey is a narrative structure that follows a protagonist through a transformative adventure, often beginning with a call to action that disrupts their ordinary world. The hero embarks on a journey filled with trials, allies, and enemies, leading to a crucial ordeal or crisis that challenges them at the core. After overcoming this central conflict, the hero gains new insight or power and returns to their familiar world, often transformed and carrying newfound wisdom or a boon that benefits others. This journey, popularized by Joseph Campbell, is a timeless framework used in storytelling across cultures and genres, symbolizing the universal process of personal growth and self-discovery.

- **Freytag's Pyramid:** This structure focuses on the rise and fall of dramatic tension throughout the story. It emphasizes the importance of a strong climax and a satisfying resolution. Freytag's Pyramid is a framework that outlines a five-part structure for dramatic storytelling. Named after Gustav Freytag, a 19th-century German novelist, this model maps out the narrative arc, guiding writers in crafting stories that align with the rhythm of human experience.

Following are the stages of Frey tag's Pyramid:

(i) Exposition: The exposition is the story's opening phase, where the characters are introduced, background details are provided, and the setting is established. This stage sets the stage for the unfolding events, giving the audience a foundation to understand the story's essential elements.

(ii) Rising Action: As the story advances, the protagonist encounters a series of challenges that intensify, driving the narrative forward and heightening the tension.

(iii) Climax: The climax marks the story's pivotal moment, where the main character faces their most crucial conflict or challenge. This is the peak of tension and often determines how the story will conclude.

(iv) Falling Action: After the climax, the story enters the falling action phase, where conflicts start to resolve, and the narrative begins to wind down. This phase allows for reflection, as the characters deal with the consequences of the climax and their actions.

(v) Denouement: The denouement, or resolution, is the narrative's final stage, where all remaining loose ends are resolved, offering closure to the story and sometimes providing insight into the characters' future.

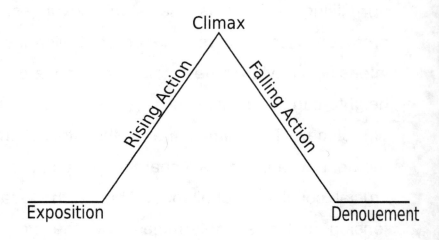

Image: Freytag's Pyramid

- **Save the Cat!:** This contemporary approach focuses on specific "beats" or key plot points that keep the audience engaged and propel the story forward. "Save the Cat!" is a screenwriting term coined by Blake Snyder and refers to a particular plot device. This method involves having the protagonist do something admirable toward the start of the story in order to establish them as a likable person and get the audience on their side.

Exploring Different Options: Familiarize yourself with various narrative frameworks, but remember, they are guidelines, not rigid rules. The best structure for your story comes from understanding your characters, plot, and the overall message you want to convey.

3.4 Case Study: The Power of Structure - "Spirited Away"

Let's revisit our previous example of "Spirited Away." This film masterfully uses the three-act structure to tell the story of Chihiro, a young girl who must find her courage and save her parents in a fantastical spirit world. Act 1 introduces Chihiro and her initial conflict (being trapped in the spirit world). Act 2 explores her challenges and growth as she works for the witch Yubaba. Finally, Act 3 brings a satisfying resolution where Chihiro overcomes her fears and achieves her goals.

This film demonstrates how a well-defined structure can help build tension, engage the audience, and deliver a powerful emotional impact.

3.5 Review Questions

1. Describe the difference between linear and non-linear storytelling.
2. Explain the three-act structure and its key components.
3. What are some other narrative frameworks besides the three-act structure

3.5 Review Questions

1. What is the difference between linear and non-linear storytelling? Provide an example of each.
2. Explain the three-act structure. What are the key elements of each act?
3. What is the Hero's Journey? How does it differ from the three-act structure?

4. How can understanding different narrative structures help you in creating your own stories?

5. Can you combine different narrative structures in a single story? Explain.

3.6 Suggested Practical Exercises

1. **Story Analysis:** Choose a film, TV show, or video game and analyze its narrative structure. Identify the key plot points and how they fit into a specific structure (e.g., three-act, Hero's Journey).

2. **Structure Experimentation:** Write a short story or script using a non-linear structure. Experiment with different time jumps or parallel storylines.

3. **Visual Storytelling:** Create a storyboard or animatic that visually represents a linear and a non-linear narrative structure.

4. **Genre Exploration:** Choose a genre (e.g., science fiction, horror, comedy) and explore

how different narrative structures can be applied to it.

These exercises will help you develop a deeper understanding of narrative structures and how to apply them effectively in your storytelling projects.

Chapter 4: Genres and Styles: Shaping Your Story

The world of stories is vast and diverse. Just like music has different genres, storytelling does too. This chapter will explore various storytelling genres and delve into the different styles that can bring your narrative to life.

4.1 Genres: The Flavors of Storytelling

Genres are categories of stories that share similar conventions, settings, and themes. Think of them like different flavors on a menu. Each genre caters to a specific audience and evokes a particular mood. Here are some popular storytelling genres:

- **Fantasy:** This genre features fantastical elements like magic, mythical creatures, and alternate worlds. Examples include "Lord of the Rings" and "Spirited Away."
- **Science Fiction:** Sci-fi stories explore the future and the impact of technology on

humanity. Think of "Star Wars" or "Blade Runner."

- **Drama:** These stories focus on serious themes like love, loss, and social issues. Examples include "The Lion King" or "Grave of the Fireflies."
- **Comedy:** Comedy stories aim to make the audience laugh. They can range from lighthearted slapstick to witty satire. Think of "The Incredibles" or "Rick and Morty."
- **Mystery:** These stories center around a crime or puzzle that needs to be solved. Examples include "Sherlock Holmes" or "Scooby-Doo."
- **Thriller:** Thrillers keep audiences on the edge of their seats with suspense, danger, and excitement. Think of "Parasite" or "Inception."

Beyond the Basics

Remember, genres aren't always clear-cut. Many stories can blend elements from different genres. For example, a story can be a science fiction mystery or a fantasy comedy.

Choosing Your Genre:

The genre you choose will depend on your story's themes, tone, and target audience. Consider what kind of experience you want to create for your viewers and choose a genre that aligns with your goals.

Image: *A visual representation of different genres*

4.2 Styles: The Voice of Your Story

While genres categorize the "what" of your story, narrative style focuses on the "how." This refers to the voice and perspective you use to tell your story. Here are some common narrative styles:

- **First-Person:** The story is narrated from the perspective of a single character using "I" statements. This creates a sense of intimacy and allows viewers to experience the story through the character's eyes. Example: "The Hunger Games."

- **Third-Person Limited:** In this style, the story is narrated from an outside perspective, but it follows the thoughts and feelings of a single character. This offers some distance but still allows viewers to connect with the protagonist. Example: "Harry Potter" series.

- **Third-Person Omniscient:** This style provides a god's-eye view of the story, allowing the narrator access to the thoughts and feelings of multiple characters. This style can be useful for complex narratives with multiple storylines. Example: "Game of Thrones."

Other stylistic choices:

- **Dialogue:** Dialogue is how characters communicate with each other. Effective dialogue can reveal character personalities, advance the plot, and create a sense of realism.

- **Description:** Descriptive writing helps bring your story's world and characters to life. Strong descriptions paint a clear picture in the reader/viewer's mind.

- **Pacing:** Pacing refers to the speed at which the story unfolds. A fast-paced story keeps the audience engaged, while a slow-paced story can create suspense or build atmosphere.

Finding Your Voice:

Experiment and find the style that best suits your story. Consider the tone you want to create, the level of intimacy you want with your audience, and the information you need to convey.

4.3 Case Study: Genre and Style in Action - "Spider-Man: Into the Spider-Verse"

Image: Poster of Spider-Man: Into the Spider-Verse (Courtesy: Marvel.com)

"Spider-Man: Into the Spider-Verse" offers a compelling example of genre and style working in tandem. The story blends science fiction with superhero elements, creating a unique and visually stunning world. The animation style is dynamic and playful, reflecting the film's energetic tone. The first-person narration from Miles Morales, the protagonist, creates a sense of immediacy and draws viewers into his journey. This film illustrates how genre and style can be harnessed to create a truly immersive and engaging storytelling experience.

4.4 Review Questions

1. What are storytelling genres? Give some examples.
2. How can understanding different genres help you craft your story?

3. Explain the difference between first-person, third-person limited, and third-person omniscient narrative styles.
4. How does style contribute to the overall tone and atmosphere of a story?
5. Can you combine different narrative styles within a single story? Explain with an example.

4.5 Suggested Practical Exercises

1. Genre Exploration: Choose a genre you are unfamiliar with and research its key characteristics. Develop a short story outline or treatment based on that genre.
2. Style Experimentation: Write a short scene from the same story using three different narrative styles: first-person, third-person limited, and third-person omniscient. Compare the effects of each style on the reader's experience.
3. Genre Mash-up: Combine two unexpected genres (e.g., horror and romance, fantasy and crime) and develop a concept for a story.

4. Character Voice: Choose a character from a well-known story and write a diary entry or social media post from their perspective.
5. Genre Analysis: Analyze a film or TV show and identify its primary genre and narrative style. Discuss how these elements contribute to the overall impact of the story.

These exercises will help you experiment with different genres and styles, expanding your storytelling toolkit and developing a deeper understanding of how to craft compelling narratives.

Chapter 5: Audience and Purpose: Knowing Who You're Telling Your Story To

Every great story starts with a purpose and a target audience in mind. In this chapter, we'll explore how understanding your audience and the message you want to convey will shape your storytelling approach.

5.1 Knowing Your Audience: Who Are You Telling Your Story To?

The success of your story hinges on connecting with your viewers. Before you put pen to paper (or stylus to tablet), take some time to define your target audience. Here are some factors to consider:

- **Age:** Are you targeting children, teenagers, adults, or a broader range of ages?
- **Interests:** What are your audience's hobbies and passions?
- **Background:** Consider your audience's cultural background and knowledge base.

- **Needs and Expectations:** What are your viewers hoping to gain from your story? Entertainment, education, emotional connection?

Understanding your audience can help you:

- **Develop relatable characters:** Create characters that resonate with your viewers' experiences and emotions.
- **Craft engaging dialogue:** Use language and humor that your audience understands and appreciates.
- **Choose the right tone and style:** Tailor your storytelling approach to the age and maturity level of your target audience.

Image: A visual to depict audience, a diverse group of people of different ages and backgrounds watching a movie screen.

5.2 Purpose and Message: What Do You Want Them to Feel or Remember?

Every story needs a reason for being. Think about the message you want to convey with your film, animation, or multimedia project. This could be:

- **Entertainment:** Pure entertainment is a perfectly valid goal.
- **Education:** Aim to inform and educate your audience on a specific topic.
- **Social Change:** Spark discussion and promote positive change on social issues.
- **Emotional Connection:** Evoke emotions like laughter, sadness, hope, or inspiration.

Having a clear purpose will guide your storytelling decisions:

- **Plot and Theme:** Align your plot and themes to your chosen message.
- **Character Development:** Develop characters who embody or represent your message.
- **Emotional Impact:** Use your story to evoke the desired emotional response in your audience.

Storytelling with Impact:

Animations and multimedia projects have the power to reach a wide audience and make a lasting impression. Being intentional about your purpose can elevate your storytelling and create a project that resonates with viewers on a deeper level.

5.3 Case Study: Purposeful Storytelling - "Wall-E"

Image: Poster of WallE (Courtesy: Walt Disney Pictures)

Disney's "Wall-E" serves as a compelling example of purposeful storytelling. The film uses a captivating robot love story to deliver a powerful message about environmentalism and consumerism. The animation style beautifully portrays a polluted Earth, while the main characters, Wall-E and Eve, evoke empathy and compassion. "Wall-E" demonstrates how animation can entertain and inform while raising important social questions.

5.4 Review Questions

1. Why is it important to consider your audience when crafting a story?
2. What are some key factors to consider when identifying your target audience?
3. How can understanding your audience help you develop a more effective story?
4. Discuss the importance of having a clear purpose for your story.
5. Can you think of an example of how animation has been used to deliver a social message?

5.5 Suggested Practical Exercises

1. **Audience Profile:** Choose a story idea and develop a detailed profile of your target audience.
2. **Elevator Pitch:** Craft a concise pitch for your story idea, focusing on your target audience and the message you want to convey.
3. **Purposeful Animation:** Find a short animation online and analyze its purpose. Identify the message or theme the animation is conveying
4. **Social Commentary:** Develop a storyboard for a short animation that addresses a social issue.
5. **Genre and Purpose:** Choose a genre and social issue. Brainstorm story ideas that combine the chosen genre with a message about the social issue.

By completing these exercises, you'll gain valuable practice in considering your audience and purpose while developing your storytelling skills.

Chapter 6: Case Studies: Learning from Storytelling Masters

Throughout history, animation and multimedia have produced countless captivating stories. This chapter delves into the power of storytelling by analyzing successful multimedia projects and exploring the impact they've had on audiences.

6.1 Dissecting Storytelling Gems

By dissecting successful projects, we can gain valuable insights into the art of storytelling. Here are some key areas to consider:

- **Target Audience:** Who is the story aimed at? How does the storytelling approach cater to their interests and expectations?

- **Narrative Structure:** What structure is used? Does it follow a classic three-act structure or employ a more non-linear format?

- **Character Development:** How are the characters developed? Are they relatable and well-rounded?

- **Theme and Purpose:** What is the underlying message of the story? How is the message conveyed through visuals, dialogue, and plot?
- **Emotional Impact:** How does the story make you feel? Does it evoke laughter, sadness, or inspire you to take action?

Image: Various key areas to be considered while developing a Multimedia Story

6.2 Popular Stories and Their Enduring Legacy

Let's delve deeper by exploring some specific examples of animation and multimedia projects that have captivated audiences and left a lasting impact:

Case Study 1: "The Lion King" (1994)

This Disney classic utilizes a timeless coming-of-age story with themes of loss, responsibility, and finding your place in the world. The animation is visually stunning, and the musical score adds emotional depth. "The Lion King" effectively uses the hero's journey narrative framework to tell a story that resonates with viewers of all ages.

Image: Poster of The Lion King (1994), Courtesy: Walt Disney Pictures

Case Study 2: "Portal" (2007)

This innovative video game combines puzzle-solving with a compelling narrative. The story unfolds through subtle environmental details and clever dialogue from an unseen AI companion. "Portal" demonstrates the power of storytelling in a non-linear format and how interactive elements can enhance the narrative experience.

Image: Portal (2007) Game. Courtesy: imdb.com

Case Study 3: "Sesame Street" (1969 - Present)

This educational children's program has been a cornerstone in storytelling for young audiences for decades. Sesame Street uses a variety of animation techniques, live-action segments, and catchy songs to teach children about letters, numbers, and social-emotional skills. It highlights the power of animation to educate and entertain at the same time.

These are just a few examples. There are countless other projects that offer lessons in storytelling. As you explore animation and multimedia, actively analyze and learn from successful narratives.

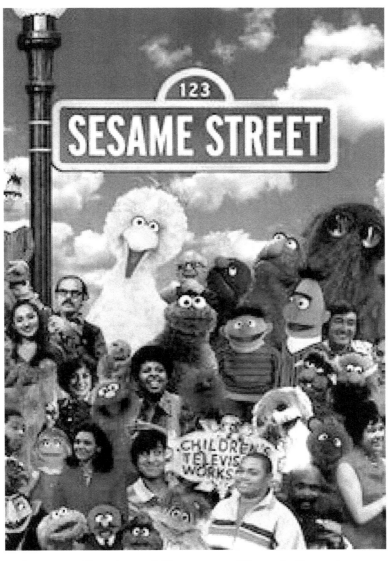

Image: Poster of Sesame Street. Courtesy:

imdb.com

6.3 Review Questions

1. Why is it valuable to analyze successful storytelling examples?
2. What are some key aspects to consider when dissecting a story in animation or multimedia?
3. Discuss the impact of "The Lion King" on audiences. How does its storytelling contribute to its success?
4. How does "Portal" use storytelling in a unique way?
5. What makes "Sesame Street" such an effective educational program?

6.4 Suggested Practical Exercises

1. **Storytelling Deconstruction:** Choose an animation or multimedia project you admire. Analyze it using the framework provided in section 6.1. Write a short report outlining your findings.
2. **Modern Reimagining:** Select a classic story and imagine how you would adapt it for a

modern audience using animation or another multimedia platform.

3. **Interactive Storytelling:** Develop a storyboard for a short interactive story that utilizes animation and user input to tell its narrative.

4. **Cross-Media Analysis:** Compare and contrast the storytelling techniques used in a film adaptation and its source material (e.g., book, video game).

By engaging with these exercises, you'll refine your analytical skills, develop your own storytelling voice, and gain a deeper appreciation for the power of storytelling in animation and multimedia.

Story

Module I: Introduction to Storytelling

Story Title: "The Lost Village"

Story Concept:

This story focuses on the fundamental elements of storytelling, such as setting, characters, conflict, and resolution, which are likely introduced in the first chapter.

The Lost Village

In a remote corner of the world, nestled deep within a dense forest, there was a village that did not appear on any map. The village of Eldoria was a place of peace and prosperity, where the villagers lived in harmony with nature and each other. However, Eldoria had a secret—it could only be found by those who truly needed it.

One day, a traveler named Mira, who had lost everything in a terrible storm, found herself wandering aimlessly through the forest. Cold, hungry, and on the brink of despair, Mira stumbled upon an ancient, overgrown path that led her to the gates of Eldoria. As she entered the village, she was welcomed warmly by the villagers, who offered her food, shelter, and kindness.

Mira quickly noticed that Eldoria was different from any place she had ever been. The village was full of life, with children playing in the streets, gardens overflowing with fruits and vegetables, and animals that seemed almost magical in their intelligence and grace. Despite her initial happiness, Mira couldn't shake a feeling of unease. The villagers never spoke of the world beyond the forest, and there were no paths leading out of the village.

One night, while exploring the village, Mira came across an old woman sitting by a fire, spinning tales of Eldoria's past. The woman revealed that Eldoria *was protected by a powerful enchantment. It could only be found by those who were lost or in need, and once someone entered, they could never leave.*

Mira was horrified. She didn't want to stay in Eldoria forever; she wanted to return to the world outside and find her way back to the life she had lost. The old woman, sensing Mira's turmoil, offered her a choice. Mira could stay in Eldoria, where she would be safe and content, or she could leave, but she would have to find her way out of the forest alone, with no guarantee of success.

After a night of restless sleep, Mira made her decision. At dawn, she bid farewell to the villagers and set out on her journey back through the forest. The path was treacherous, and Mira faced many challenges, but she never gave up. She knew that the only way to find herself again was to leave Eldoria behind.

As Mira walked, the forest began to thin, and the sunlight grew brighter. Finally, she emerged from the trees and found herself on a familiar road. Though tired and worn, Mira felt a renewed sense of purpose. She had been lost, but now she was found.

Eldoria faded into the mists of memory, a place that existed only for those who truly needed it. Mira continued her journey, carrying with her the lessons of Eldoria—of hope, resilience, and the courage to find her own path.

Analysis: This story exemplifies the key components of storytelling discussed in the first chapter. It introduces a setting (the village of Eldoria), characters (Mira, the old woman), a central conflict (Mira's decision to stay or leave), and a resolution (Mira's choice to leave and the lessons she learns). The story is simple yet effective in demonstrating how these elements work together to create a compelling narrative.

Module II
Character Development

Chapter 7: Creating Memorable Characters: The Soul of Your Story

Characters are the heart and soul of any story. They drive the plot forward, evoke emotions in the audience, and leave a lasting impression. In this chapter, we'll delve into the world of character development, exploring the traits of compelling characters and the roles they play in your narrative.

7.1 The Power of Compelling Characters

Memorable characters make your story come alive. They are relatable, engaging, and capable of sparking an emotional connection with the audience. When viewers care about your characters, they become invested in their journeys, making the story more impactful.

What Makes a Character Compelling?

- **Desires and Goals:** Every character should have something they want or strive to achieve. This gives them purpose and drives their actions.

- **Flaws and Challenges:** No one is perfect. Flawed characters are more relatable and interesting to follow. Challenges help them grow and change throughout the story.
- **Motivation:** What drives your characters? Is it love, revenge, a desire for justice? Understanding their motivations helps the audience connect with their choices.
- **Voice and Personality:** Give your characters a distinct voice and personality. How do they speak? How do they react to situations?
- **Visual Design (for animation):** In animation and multimedia, visual design plays a crucial role in character development. The character's appearance and animation style should reflect their personality and inner world.

Image: A collage of different characters with distinct personalities and appearances.

7.2 The Cast of Characters: Protagonists, Antagonists, and Supporting Players

Every story needs a cast of characters to populate its world. Here are the key roles:

- **Protagonist:** The hero or main character, who drives the story forward and faces the greatest challenges.
- **Antagonist:** The villain or opposing force who creates conflict and obstacles for the protagonist.
- **Supporting Characters:** These characters play a vital role in the protagonist's journey. They can be friends, mentors, allies, or even foils.

(A foil is a character in a story who contrasts with another character, typically the protagonist, to highlight particular qualities or traits of that character. This contrast can help to develop themes or deepen the understanding of the characters' motivations. In literature, foils are used to emphasize differences in personality, behavior, or values.)

Beyond the Basics:

Character roles can be more complex than just hero and villain. Anti-heroes are flawed protagonists with questionable morals. Supporting characters can have their own storylines that intersect with the main plot. The key is to create a diverse and engaging cast that contributes to the overall narrative.

7.3 Case Study: Character Chemistry - "Inside Out"

Disney's "Inside Out" offers a compelling example of well-developed characters. The film takes viewers inside the mind of a young girl, Riley, where her emotions – Joy, Sadness, Anger, Fear, and Disgust – are personified as characters. Each emotion has a distinct personality, design, and role in Riley's emotional journey. Their interactions and conflicts highlight the importance of all emotions and the complex inner workings of the human mind. "Inside Out" demonstrates how strong character development can elevate a story and make it resonate with audiences of all ages.

7.4 Review Questions

1. Why are well-developed characters crucial for a successful story?

2. What are some key elements of a compelling character?

3. Explain the differences between protagonists, antagonists, and supporting characters.

4. Discuss how character design can contribute to character development in animation.

5. How does "Inside Out" use character development to explore a complex concept?

7.5 Suggested Practical Exercises

1. **Character Profile:** Choose a character from a story you admire and create a detailed profile outlining their goals, motivations, flaws, and personality traits.

2. **Character Voice Exercise:** Write a short dialogue scene between two characters. Focus on capturing their unique voices and personalities through their dialogue and actions.

3. **Character Redesign:** Select a popular character and redesign them for a different

genre. Consider how their appearance and personality might change to fit the new setting.

4. **Character Flaw Exploration:** Choose a character with a prominent flaw and brainstorm ways to overcome that flaw throughout the story.

5. **Character Relationship Map:** Develop a visual map that outlines the relationships between different characters in your story.

By engaging in these exercises, you'll gain valuable practice in crafting memorable characters that will drive your stories forward and leave a lasting impression on your audience.

Chapter 8: Character Arcs and Growth: Shaping Your Characters' Journeys

Compelling characters aren't static figures. They evolve and grow throughout your story, facing challenges and learning valuable lessons. This chapter explores the concept of character arcs, the journeys your characters take as the narrative unfolds.

8.1 The Importance of Character Arcs

Characters who grow and change over the course of your story feel more realistic and engaging. They leave a lasting impression on the audience as viewers connect with their triumphs and struggles. A well-defined character arc strengthens your narrative in several ways:

- **Raises the Stakes:** As characters change, the stakes of the story can rise. Their journey becomes more personal and emotionally resonant.

- **Creates Conflict:** Character growth often involves overcoming internal conflicts and challenges. This creates tension and keeps the audience engaged.
- **Offers Themes and Messages:** The changes your characters undergo can embody the themes and messages of your story.

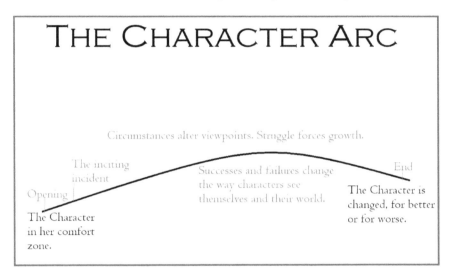

THE CHARACTER ARC

Circumstances alter viewpoints. Struggle forces growth.

The inciting incident

Opening

The Character in her comfort zone.

Successes and failures change the way characters see themselves and their world.

End

The Character is changed, for better or for worse.

Image: A visual representation of a character arc showing a character's starting point, a point of transformation, and their final point.

8.2 Types of Character Arcs

There are various types of character arcs, each offering a unique approach to character development:

- **Transformation Arc:** This is the most classic type. The character starts in one place, undergoes a significant change, and emerges a different person by the end.
- **Coming of Age Arc:** This arc focuses on a young character's journey into adulthood. They learn valuable lessons, gain independence, and confront the challenges of growing up.
- **Redemption Arc:** A flawed character seeks to atone for their past mistakes and become a better person.
- **Fall from Grace Arc:** A once-noble character succumbs to temptation or tragedy, leading to their downfall.
- **Static Arc:** While less common, some characters may not undergo significant changes. This can work if the story focuses on

a specific event or situation rather than character development.

Choosing the Right Arc:

The best character arc for your story depends on your character's starting point, goals, and the overall narrative. Consider the theme you want to convey and how your character's journey can contribute to it.

8.3 Case Study: A Journey of Transformation - "Spirited Away"

Hayao Miyazaki's film "Spirited Away" provides a powerful example of a transformative character arc. Chihiro, a young girl, enters the spirit world and gets trapped, forced to work for a witch. Initially scared and self-centered, Chihiro is forced to confront her fears and learn important lessons about courage, independence, and compassion. Through her struggles and experiences, Chihiro undergoes a significant transformation, emerging from the spirit world a braver and more mature young woman. This character arc strengthens the story's themes of self-discovery and facing adversity.

Image: Poster of Spirited Away (2001). Courtesy imdb.com

8.4 Review Questions

1. Why is character growth important in storytelling?

2. Explain how a well-defined character arc can strengthen your narrative.

3. Describe the different types of character arcs.

4. How does Chihiro's character arc contribute to the overall message of "Spirited Away"?

5. When might a static character arc be an effective choice in storytelling?

8.5 Suggested Practical Exercises

1. **Character Arc Mapping:** Choose a character from a story and map their journey throughout the narrative. Identify their starting point, challenges, turning points, and final state.

2. **Reimagining an Arc:** Select a character with a static arc and rewrite their story, creating a transformative arc for them.

3. **Genre and Arc Exploration:** Consider a specific genre (e.g., sci-fi, comedy) and explore how different types of character arcs might be used within that genre.

4. **Thematic Storytelling:** Choose a theme for your story and develop a character arc that embodies that theme.

5. **Character Motivation and Growth:** Analyze a character's initial motivations and desires. Brainstorm how these motivations could drive their growth and transformation throughout the story.

By working through these exercises, you'll gain a deeper understanding of character arcs, allowing you to craft compelling characters who not only drive your story forward but also resonate with your audience on a deeper level.

Chapter 9: Dialogue and Interaction: Bringing Your Characters to Life

Dialogue and interaction are the lifeblood of storytelling. They are how your characters reveal their personalities, advance the plot, and forge connections with each other and the audience. This chapter delves into the art of writing authentic dialogue and crafting engaging character interactions.

9.1 Writing Dialogue that Rings True

Effective dialogue sounds natural and believable. Here are some key elements to consider:

- **Voice and Personality:** Every character should have a distinct voice that reflects their personality, age, background, and social status.

- **Subtext and Emotion:** Dialogue isn't just about what characters say, but also what they imply. Use subtext and emotional delivery to add depth and meaning.

- **Action and Description:** Intersperse dialogue with action and description to break up the text and provide context about body language and setting.
- **Clarity and Concision:** Keep your dialogue clear and concise. Avoid overly complex vocabulary or flowery language unless it suits a specific character.

mage: *A visual representation of different character personalities reflected in different speech bubble styles.*

9.2 The Power of Interaction

Beyond words, how characters interact with each other shapes the narrative. Here are some aspects to consider:

- **Conflict and Tension:** Not all interactions are friendly. Conflict and disagreements can create tension and keep the audience engaged.

- **Collaboration and Support:** Show how characters work together to overcome challenges. This reinforces character relationships and highlights teamwork.

- **Non-verbal Communication:** Body language, facial expressions, and gestures are crucial for conveying emotions and subtext without words.

- **Dialogue Styles:** Vary your dialogue styles. Use banter for lighthearted moments, witty exchanges for humor, and dramatic monologues for emotional impact.

Beyond the Basics:

Dialogue and interaction can also showcase your understanding of different cultures, social situations, and power dynamics. Use these elements to create a rich and believable world for your story.

9.3 Case Study: The Art of Conversation - "The Incredibles"

Brad Bird's "The Incredibles" showcases the power of dialogue and interaction. The film uses humor and witty banter to depict the family dynamic of the Parr family of superheroes. We see their individual personalities come alive through their interactions, highlighting not just their powers but also their flaws and vulnerabilities. Even during action sequences, dialogue is used to convey strategy, emotions, and character development. "The Incredibles" demonstrates how well-written dialogue and interaction can enrich the storytelling experience.

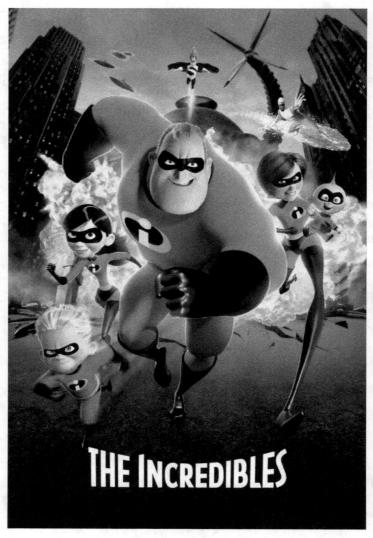

Image: Poster of The Incredibles (2004).

Courtesy: www.themoviedb.org

9.4 Review Questions

1. Why is creating realistic and engaging dialogue important in storytelling?
2. What are some key elements to consider when writing dialogue?
3. How can character interactions be used to advance the plot and develop relationships?
4. Discuss the importance of non-verbal communication in animation and multimedia.
5. How does "The Incredibles" use dialogue and interaction to flesh out its characters and world?

9.5 Suggested Practical Exercises

1. **Character Dialogue Practice:** Choose two characters from your story and write a dialogue scene that showcases their personalities and relationship.
2. **Emotional Delivery:** Write a short scene using minimal dialogue but strong emotional delivery through action and description.
3. **Subtext and Secrets:** Write a dialogue scene with underlying subtext or hidden information

that one character is trying to convey to another.

4. **Genre Exploration:** Research how dialogue styles differ across different genres (e.g., fantasy, science fiction). Write a short scene exploring this variation.

5. **Non-verbal Storytelling:** Create a storyboard depicting a scene that relies solely on non-verbal communication to tell the story.

By engaging in these exercises, you'll gain valuable practice in crafting authentic characters, writing natural dialogue, and using interaction to create a compelling narrative.

Chapter 10: Character Design in Animation: Bringing Your Characters to Life Visually

In animation, character design goes beyond just creating a pretty picture. It's about breathing life into your characters, visually communicating their personality, and complementing the narrative. This chapter explores the principles of animation character design and how it integrates with storytelling.

10.1 Visual Design Principles for Animated Characters

A well-designed animated character should be visually engaging, memorable, and easy to read. Here are some key design principles to consider:

- **Shape and Form:** Use basic shapes like circles, squares, and triangles to construct your character's body. This simplifies their form and makes them easier to animate.

- **Proportion and Scale:** Consider realistic human proportions for human characters or exaggerate features for comedic effect or to convey specific personality traits.
- **Silhouette:** A strong silhouette allows your character to be recognizable even from a distance or against a busy background.
- **Color Theory:** Choose colors that reflect your character's personality, mood, and role in the story. Warm colors like red and orange suggest activity and energy, while cool colors like blue and green convey calmness or mystery.
- **Line and Detail:** Strikes a balance between detail and simplicity. Too much detail can be distracting in animation. Use lines to define form, movement, and facial expressions.

Image: A visual showcasing different character designs with varying shapes, proportions, silhouettes, and color palettes.

10.2 Integrating Visual and Narrative Elements

Character design should not exist in isolation. It should seamlessly integrate with the narrative elements of your story:

- **Personality and Emotion:** The visual design of your character should reflect their personality and inner world. Clothing, facial features, and body language all contribute to this.
- **Role in the Story:** Is your character a hero, villain, or sidekick? Their design should hint at their role in the narrative.
- **Genre and World:** The genre and setting of your story should be reflected in the character designs. For example, a character in a dark fantasy world would have a different design than one in a whimsical children's cartoon.

Image: A comparison of contrasting character designs from different genres (e.g., fantasy vs. sci-fi) to highlight how visual elements reflect the world and story.

10.3 Case Study: Visually Captivating Characters - "Spider-Man: Into the Spider-Verse"

The animated film "Spider-Man: Into the Spider-Verse" excels in its innovative character design. Each character within the film's multiverse has a distinct visual style, reflecting their personality and origin story. Miles Morales' design blends street art and comic book elements, emphasizing his youthful energy and Brooklyn roots. Peter B. Parker's design uses muted colors and a slightly slumped posture, showcasing his worn-down demeanor. The film demonstrates how character design can be a powerful storytelling tool, enriching the narrative and creating a visually captivating experience.

Image: Poster of Spider-Man: Into the Spider-Verse

(2018) Courtesy: www.themoviedb.org

10.4 Review Questions

1. Why is character design crucial in animation beyond just aesthetics?

2. Explain the importance of visual design principles like shape, proportion, and color in character creation.

3. How can the visual design of a character reflect their personality and role in the story?

4. Discuss the impact of genre and setting on character design.

5. Analyze how "Spider-Man: Into the Spider-Verse" uses character design to enhance its storytelling.

10.5 Suggested Practical Exercises

1. **Character Design Challenge:** Choose a character from your story and create three different character design variations exploring different shapes, colors, and styles.

2. **Personality Through Design:** Select an existing character and redesign them to reflect a completely different personality.

3. **Genre Swap:** Design a character for a specific genre (e.g., sci-fi, fantasy). Then, redesign them to fit a completely different genre.

4. **Mood and Emotion:** Create a series of character sketches showcasing how different choices in color, line, and facial expression can convey varying emotions.

5. **Storyboard Analysis:** Analyze a storyboard from an animated film and identify how character design is used to communicate personality, role, and story elements.

By engaging in these exercises, you'll refine your visual design skills, learn to translate narrative elements into character appearance, and discover the power of character design in animation storytelling.

Chapter 11: Case Studies: Learning from Animated Legends

Throughout animation history, countless films and multimedia projects have brought unforgettable characters to life. This chapter delves deeper into character development by analyzing well-constructed characters from animation and multimedia.

11.1 Deconstructing Character Complexity

By dissecting these characters, we can gain valuable insights into the art of creating compelling figures that resonate with audiences. Here's what to consider:

- **Motivation and Goals:** What drives the character? What are they trying to achieve? Understanding their motivations helps us connect with their actions and journey.

- **Flaws and Challenges:** No one is perfect. Flawed characters are more relatable and interesting to follow. Challenges help them grow and change throughout the story.

- **Relationships and Interactions:** How does the character interact with others? These interactions reveal their personality, vulnerabilities, and value system.

- **Visual Design and Animation:** In animation, visual design plays a crucial role in character development. Explore how the character's appearance and animation style support their personality and narrative arc.

- **Cultural Impact:** Certain characters become iconic and transcend their original stories. Analyze why these characters resonate with audiences across cultures and generations.

Image: A collage showcasing diverse animated characters from different genres and eras.

11.2 Case Studies: A Gallery of Memorable Characters

Case Study 1: Wall-E (Disney/Pixar, 2008)

Wall-E, the adorable waste-compacting robot, captures hearts with his unwavering determination and childlike curiosity. Despite limited dialogue, his actions and expressions effectively convey his loneliness, love for Eve, and desire for a better world. Wall-E's character arc highlights the importance of connection and perseverance, offering a message that resonates with viewers of all ages.

Image: Poster of Wall E movie. Courtesy: Disney Pixar.

Case Study 2: Coraline (Laika, 2009)

Coraline Jones is a spunky and independent protagonist who takes charge in a fantastical yet unsettling world. Her resourcefulness, curiosity, and refusal to back down in the face of danger make her a relatable and empowering character. Coraline's journey exemplifies the importance of bravery, self-reliance, and confronting one's fears.

Image: Caroline. Courtesy Laika.com

Case Study 3: Iroh (Avatar: The Last Airbender, Nickelodeon, 2005-2008)

Uncle Iroh from "Avatar: The Last Airbender" embodies wisdom, compassion, and inner strength. He serves as a mentor figure to the protagonist, Prince Zuko, offering guidance and encouragement while grappling with his own past mistakes. Iroh's character demonstrates the power of redemption and the importance of finding inner peace.

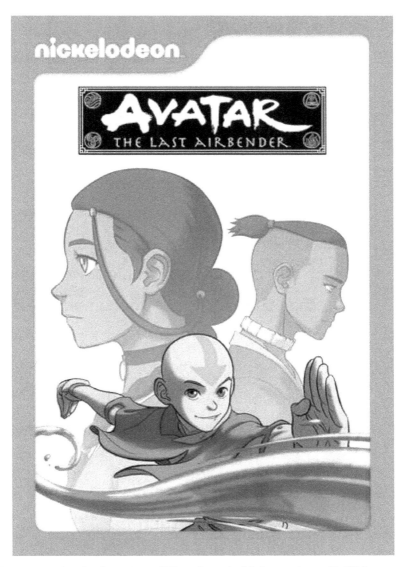

Image: Iroh Avatar: The Last Airbender, IMDb.com

11.3 Review Questions

1. What can we learn by analyzing well-developed characters in animation?
2. Discuss the importance of motivation, flaws, and relationships in character development.
3. How does animation use visual design and animation style to enhance character development?
4. Select one of the case studies and analyze why the character has become culturally impactful.
5. Can you name another character from animation or multimedia that you find compelling? Explain what makes them so engaging.

11.4 Suggested Practical Exercises

1. **Character Deconstruction:** Choose a favorite animated character and analyze them using the factors listed in section 11.1. Write a detailed character profile highlighting their

motivations, flaws, relationships, and visual design.

2. **Character Reimagining:** Select a character and reimagine them in a different setting or genre. How might their personality, motivations, and goals change?

3. **Character from Scratch:** Develop a new character for a specific genre. Create a backstory, personality traits, and a visual design that reflects their role in your story.

4. **Dialogue Analysis:** Choose a scene between two characters from an animated film. Analyze how their dialogue reveals their personalities, motivations, and the nature of their relationship.

5. **Character Arc Brainstorming:** Develop a character concept with a clear starting point and a potential flaw. Brainstorm challenges and events that could lead to a significant transformation for this character.

By working through these exercises, you'll gain valuable experience in understanding and creating impactful characters that will drive your stories forward and leave a lasting impression on your audience.

Chapter 12: Workshop: Bringing Your Characters to Life

Now that you've explored the principles of character development, it's time to put your knowledge into practice! This chapter serves as a workshop, guiding you through the process of creating and fleshing out characters for your own animation or multimedia project.

12.1 Brainstorming Your Cast

Before diving into specific characters, consider the overall arc of your story. What kind of characters will best drive your narrative and engage your audience? Here are some brainstorming techniques:

- **Role-Playing:** Identify the key roles in your story (protagonist, antagonist, helpers, etc.) and try role-playing them to explore their personalities and motivations.

- **Character Inspiration:** Draw inspiration from real people, historical figures, myths, or even existing fictional characters (with a unique twist!).

- **Genre Specific:** Certain genres have character archetypes (e.g., the wise mentor in fantasy). Brainstorm within these archetypes while adding your own creative spin.

Image: A character coming out of a flow, depicting brainstorming techniques for character development.

12.2 Building Your Characters: A Step-by-Step Guide

Let's delve into crafting individual characters. Here's a step-by-step approach to guide you:

Step 1: Character Name and Basic Description

Give your character a name that reflects their personality or role in the story. Briefly describe their appearance, age, and occupation.

Step 2: Motivation and Desires

What drives your character? What do they want to achieve? Understanding their desires creates a foundation for their journey.

Step 3: Flaws and Challenges

No one is perfect. What are your character's flaws? How do these flaws create challenges they must overcome?

Step 4: Relationships

How does your character interact with others? These interactions reveal their personality, values, and how they navigate the world.

Step 5: Voice and Personality

How does your character speak? Are they sarcastic, timid, or assertive? Develop a distinct voice that reflects their personality.

Step 6: Visual Design (for animation)

If your project is animation, create a visual design that complements your character's personality and role.

Step 7: Character Arc

Consider a potential character arc. How will your character change and grow throughout the story?

12.3 Case Study: Student Project Success - "The Misplaced Martians"

A student team at [insert a relevant college name] created an animated short film titled "The Misplaced Martians." The story follows two hapless Martian explorers who land on Earth by mistake. The team developed distinct personalities for their characters.

Zork, the leader, is arrogant and impulsive, while Blop, his assistant, is timid and cautious. These contrasting personalities fueled humor and created tension as they navigated Earth's unfamiliar challenges. This case study demonstrates how strong character development can elevate a student project, creating engaging narratives and memorable experiences for the audience.

(Martian: hypothetical inhabitants of the planet Mars)

12.4 Review Questions

1. Why is it important to develop a well-rounded cast of characters for your project?

2. Describe different techniques for brainstorming character ideas.

3. Walk through the steps you would take to build a character profile.

4. How can character flaws and challenges be used to create a compelling narrative arc?

5. Discuss the role of voice and personality in character development.

12.5 Suggested Practical Exercises

1. **Character Brainstorming Session:** Gather your classmates and brainstorm ideas for characters for a class project. Utilize different techniques like role-playing or brainstorming based on genre archetypes.

2. **Character Profile Development:** Choose one of the characters you brainstormed and develop a detailed profile, following the step-by-step guide in section 12.2. Include a visual design sketch if your project is an animation.

3. **Character Interaction Scene:** Write a short dialogue scene featuring two characters from your project. Focus on revealing their personalities, motivations, and potential conflict through their interactions.

4. **Character Arc Mapping:** Using your chosen character, map out their potential journey throughout your story. Identify their starting point, key events that challenge them, and their anticipated end state.

5. **Character Pitch:** Prepare a short pitch to your classmates introducing your character. Briefly explain their personality, motivation, and role in your story.

Story

Module II: Character Development

Story Title: "The Tale of Aiden, the Reluctant Hero"

Story Concept:

This story will illustrate the principles of character development, focusing on creating a multi-dimensional protagonist with a clear character arc, motivations, and growth throughout the narrative.

The Tale of Aiden, the Reluctant Hero

In the small, misty town of Gloomhaven, lived a young man named Aiden. Unlike the brave and daring heroes of legend, Aiden was an ordinary blacksmith's apprentice. He was quiet, reserved, and content to live a simple life, far from the dangers and adventures that others sought. However, deep within his heart, Aiden harbored a fear that he would never admit—not to anyone, and especially not to himself. Aiden feared failure.

Gloomhaven was a town overshadowed by the presence of the Dark Forest, a place of ancient evil that no one dared to enter. For centuries, the townsfolk had lived in fear of the forest's curse, but as long as they stayed within the town's borders, they were safe. Or so they believed.

One fateful day, a stranger arrived in Gloomhaven, seeking help. The stranger, an old and wise sage, revealed that the curse of the Dark Forest was spreading, slowly consuming the land. If nothing was done, Gloomhaven would be swallowed by darkness within a month. The only way to lift the curse was to retrieve a sacred artifact hidden deep within the forest.

The townspeople were terrified, and no one volunteered for the task. Aiden, standing in the crowd, felt a pang of guilt. He knew that someone had to go, but he was paralyzed by his fear of failing.

What if he wasn't strong enough? What if he couldn't find the artifact? What if he let everyone down?

That night, Aiden couldn't sleep. The weight of the townspeople's fear hung heavily on him. He remembered his father, a blacksmith who had passed away years ago. His father had always told him that true courage wasn't about being fearless; it was about doing what was right, even when you were afraid. Aiden realized that if he didn't act, the town—and everyone he cared about—would be lost.

The next morning, Aiden stepped forward and volunteered to enter the Dark Forest. The townspeople were shocked. Aiden had never shown any interest in heroics, and many doubted he could succeed. But Aiden was determined. He set off with nothing but his father's old sword and a lantern to guide his way.

The journey through the Dark Forest was perilous. Aiden faced many challenges, from treacherous terrain to sinister creatures lurking in the shadows. At every turn, his fears threatened to overwhelm him, but he pressed on, remembering his father's words.

As he ventured deeper into the forest, Aiden began to change. He learned to trust his instincts, to face his fears head-on, and to rely on his inner strength. He forged alliances with creatures of the forest who saw the goodness in his heart, and he discovered that the true source of his power was not in his physical strength, but in his courage and determination.

After many trials, Aiden finally found the sacred artifact—a glowing crystal that pulsed with ancient magic. As he grasped it, he felt a surge of power and a sense of peace. The curse began to lift, and the darkness receded from the forest.

Aiden returned to Gloomhaven a different man. He was no longer the quiet, unassuming apprentice, but a hero in his own right. The townspeople greeted him with cheers and gratitude, and Aiden realized that he had found something more valuable than the artifact—he had found his true self.

From that day on, Aiden was known as the hero of Gloomhaven, not because of his deeds, but because of the strength of character he had shown. He continued to live in the town, helping others and sharing the wisdom he had gained on his journey.

Analysis: This story demonstrates the core principles of character development, focusing on Aiden's transformation from a reluctant, fearful young man to a courageous and self-assured hero. The story highlights how a character's internal struggles, motivations, and growth can drive the narrative forward, making the character relatable and the story more engaging. Aiden's journey illustrates how external challenges can mirror and influence a character's internal development, leading to a satisfying and meaningful character arc.

Module III
Plot and Structure

Chapter 13: Plot Development: Building the Backbone of Your Story

A gripping plot is the foundation of any engaging story. It's the journey your characters take, the challenges they face, and how those experiences lead to a satisfying resolution. This chapter explores the elements of a good plot and various techniques to develop it effectively.

13.1 The Essential Ingredients of a Strong Plot

Great plots share some key elements:

- **Conflict:** This is the driving force of your story. It creates tension, keeps the audience engaged, and motivates your characters to act.
- **Rising Action:** The protagonist faces a series of escalating challenges, raising the stakes and building tension.
- **Climax:** This is the peak of the conflict, the moment of greatest tension and resolution.

- **Falling Action:** The events following the climax, leading to the final resolution of the story.
- **Resolution:** The ending of the story, where the conflict is resolved and the characters (and audience) reach a sense of closure.

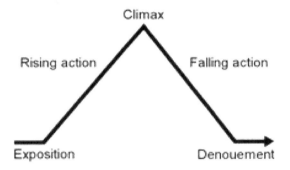

Image: A visual representation of a story arc, depicting the exposition, rising action, climax, falling action, and resolution.

Beyond the Basics:

While these elements are essential, a good plot can also incorporate subplots, twists and turns, and red herrings (false clues) to keep the audience guessing and engaged.

13.2 Techniques for Plot Development

Developing a compelling plot takes planning and creativity. Here are some helpful techniques:

- **Brainstorming:** Freely generate ideas for your story's central conflict, potential challenges, and the desired outcome. Don't be afraid of unconventional elements!

- **Mind Mapping:** Use a mind map to visually organize your ideas, connecting themes, characters, and plot points.

- **The Hero's Journey:** This classic story structure follows a hero's departure from their ordinary world, journey through challenges, and eventual return transformed. It can be a valuable framework to shape your plot.

- **Plot Point Outlining:** Develop a detailed outline of your plot, breaking it down into key scenes and events. This can help ensure your story flows logically and builds towards a satisfying conclusion.

- **Getting Feedback:** Share your plot ideas with trusted friends or advisors. Feedback can help you identify weaknesses and refine your story.

Remember: There's no single "right" way to develop a plot. Experiment, explore different structures, and find what works best for your story.

13.3 Case Study: Plotting a Masterpiece - "Spirited Away"

Hayao Miyazaki's "Spirited Away" showcases masterful plot development. Chihiro, a young girl, enters the spirit world and must work to free herself and her parents. The film expertly uses conflict (Chihiro's need to escape) and rising action (challenges she faces working for the witch Yubaba). The climax involves a daring rescue attempt, followed by a satisfying resolution where Chihiro emerges victorious and transformed. "Spirited Away" demonstrates how a well-structured plot with clear goals, escalating challenges, and a satisfying conclusion can create a captivating story.

Image: Poster of Spirited Away. Courtesy: Pinterest

13.4 Review Questions

1. Why is a strong plot crucial for effective storytelling?
2. Explain the key elements of a compelling plot structure.
3. Discuss different techniques for brainstorming and developing your plot.
4. How can the Hero's Journey structure be used to guide your plot development?
5. Analyze how "Spirited Away" uses plot elements to create a captivating story.

13.5 Suggested Practical Exercises

1. **Brainstorming Bonanza:** Set a timer and brainstorm potential plot ideas for a story in your chosen genre. Write down everything that comes to mind, no matter how outlandish it may seem.
2. **Mind Mapping Magic:** Choose one of your brainstormed ideas and create a mind map to visualize your plot's elements, characters, and potential events.

3. **The Hero's Journey Template:** Apply the Hero's Journey structure to an existing story you admire. Analyze how it aligns with the different stages of the journey.

4. **Plot Point Outlining:** Start outlining the plot for your story. Identify major sections like introduction, rising action, climax, and resolution.

5. **Peer Review and Feedback:** Share your plot outline with a classmate and discuss potential strengths and weaknesses. Offer feedback on their plot outline in return.

Chapter 14: Conflict and Resolution: The Engine and Endpoint of Your Story

Conflict is the lifeblood of any compelling story. It's the force that drives your characters, creates tension, and propels the narrative forward. This chapter delves into different types of conflict and explores how to craft satisfying resolutions that leave your audience feeling fulfilled.

14.1 The Power of Conflict

Conflict can be internal (within a character) or external (between characters or against a force). Understanding these distinctions helps you create engaging dynamics:

- **Internal Conflict:** This occurs within a character, where they struggle with emotions, desires, or beliefs. This can be a powerful tool for character development and audience connection.

- **External Conflict:** This involves an obstacle or antagonist that the protagonist must overcome. This can be anything from a physical threat to a societal injustice.

Image: A visual representation of an internal vs. external conflict. The character with a thought bubble depicting an internal struggle,

contrasted with an image of a character facing an external threat like a villain.

14.2 Crafting Compelling Conflicts

Here are some elements to consider when crafting strong conflicts:

- **Clearly Defined Goals:** What does your protagonist want? What stands in their way? A clear understanding of these goals creates a compelling conflict with stakes that matter.

- **Escalating Stakes:** As the story progresses, the consequences of failure should increase, raising the tension and urgency for the protagonist to succeed.

- **Multiple Layers:** Consider layering internal and external conflicts for richer storytelling. For example, a character facing an external enemy might also be battling their own self-doubt.

14.3 The Art of Resolution

The resolution is how your story ties up the loose ends, leaving the audience with a sense of closure. While all stories need a resolution, there's flexibility in how you achieve it:

- **Happy Ending:** The protagonist overcomes all obstacles and achieves their goals. This is a classic resolution that leaves the audience feeling satisfied and optimistic.

- **Bittersweet Ending:** The protagonist achieves some goals but at a cost. This can be a more nuanced and thought-provoking ending.

- **Open Ending:** The story concludes without definitively resolving all conflicts, leaving room for interpretation and audience discussion.

Remember: The best resolution is the one that feels most natural and satisfying for your specific story.

14.4 Case Study: Resolving Conflict with Heart - "How to Train Your Dragon"

"How to Train Your Dragon" by DreamWorks Animation showcases effective conflict resolution. Hiccup, a young Viking struggling with his own shortcomings, must overcome prejudice and a fearsome dragon to prove himself. The film employs both internal and external conflict to drive the story. Ultimately, Hiccup's courage, empathy, and resourcefulness pave the way for a happy ending, where humans and dragons learn to coexist. "How to Train Your Dragon" demonstrates how resolution can be both satisfying and impactful, fostering themes of acceptance and understanding.

Image: Poster of How to train Your Dragon.

Courtesy: Dream Works

14.5 Review Questions

1. Explain the difference between internal and external conflict. How can they be used together?

2. What are some elements to consider when crafting a compelling conflict for your story?

3. Discuss the importance of clearly defined goals and escalating stakes in creating a strong conflict.

4. What are some different types of resolutions, and when might each be appropriate?

5. Analyze how "How to Train Your Dragon" uses conflict and resolution to create a satisfying story.

14.6 Suggested Practical Exercises

1. **Conflict Brainstorming:** Develop a character and identify a potential internal conflict they might face. Then brainstorm different external conflicts they could encounter that would further challenge them.

2. **Escalating Stakes:** Choose a conflict from your story and develop a series of escalating

challenges the protagonist faces as they strive to overcome it.

3. **Resolution Options:** Brainstorm different possible resolutions for your story's central conflict. Consider a happy ending, bittersweet ending, or an open ending. Discuss which option would be most satisfying for your story and audience.

4. **Scene Rewriting:** Rewrite the climax or resolution scene of an existing story, changing the outcome to create an alternative resolution. Analyze how this change alters the overall message and tone of the story.

5. **Peer Review:** Share your conflict and resolution ideas with a classmate and discuss potential strengths and weaknesses. Offer feedback on their ideas in return.

Chapter 15: Pacing and Timing: The Rhythm of Your Story

Imagine watching a film where exciting scenes rush by one after another, leaving you breathless and confused. Or perhaps you've experienced a story that drags on endlessly, each scene feeling like an eternity. Pacing and timing are crucial elements in storytelling, dictating the flow of your narrative and keeping your audience engaged. This chapter explores the importance of pacing and offers techniques for controlling the rhythm of your story.

15.1 The Power of Pacing

Pacing refers to the speed at which your story unfolds. A well-paced story moves forward at a rate that keeps the audience engaged without feeling rushed or stagnant. Effective pacing accomplishes two key goals:

- **Maintains audience interest:** Varied pacing creates a sense of rhythm, building anticipation and excitement during suspenseful moments and allowing for slower exploration during character development or emotional scenes.

- **Enhances understanding:** A balanced pace ensures the audience has enough time to grasp information, absorb emotional beats, and connect with the characters.

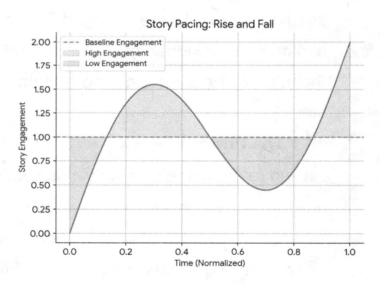

Image: A representative graph depicting a well-paced story, story represented by a line

that rises and falls, creating a dynamic
rhythm.

15.2 Techniques for Controlling Narrative Timing

So how can you influence the pace of your story? Here are some techniques to consider:

- **Scene Length:** Short, action-packed scenes can accelerate the pace, while longer scenes with dialogue or introspection can slow it down.

- **Level of Detail:** Vivid descriptions and intricate world-building can slow the pace, while concise descriptions and a focus on key actions can speed it up.

- **Dialogue:** Lengthy dialogue exchanges can slow the pace, while snappy dialogue or witty exchanges can quicken it.

- **Action and Suspense:** Fast-paced action sequences increase the sense of urgency and raise the stakes, while moments of suspense can build anticipation and slow the pace before a dramatic payoff.

- **Cliffhangers:** Ending a scene on a cliffhanger leaves the audience eager to find out what happens next, accelerating the perceived pace as they yearn for more.

Remember: There's no one-size-fits-all approach to pacing. Experiment with different techniques and find a rhythm that works for your story and genre.

15.3 Case Study: Pacing Perfection - "Spider-Man: Into the Spider-Verse"

"Spider-Man: Into the Spider-Verse" excels in its dynamic pacing. The film seamlessly blends fast-paced action sequences with humor, character development, and emotional moments. Scenes often begin with a frenetic energy, slowing down for character interactions or exposition before launching back into the action. This creates a unique rhythm that keeps the audience engaged while enriching the narrative.

Image: Poster of Spider-Man: Into the Spider Verse. Courtesy: Posterwa.com

15.4 Review Questions

1. Why is pacing crucial in storytelling?
2. What are two main goals of effective pacing?
3. Discuss different techniques for controlling the pace of your story.
4. How can the use of scene length, dialogue, and action sequences influence the pace of your narrative?
5. Analyze how "Spider-Man: Into the Spider-Verse" uses pacing to enhance its storytelling.

15.5 Suggested Practical Exercises

1. **Scene Analysis:** Select a scene from an animated film and analyze its pacing. Consider the scene length, level of detail, dialogue, and action sequences. Discuss how these elements contribute to the overall pace of the scene.

2. **Pacing Script Revision:** Choose a scene you've written and identify a pacing issue (too fast or too slow). Rewrite the scene, using techniques discussed in this chapter to adjust the pace and achieve a desired effect.

3. **Storytelling Speed Test:** Write a short scene that conveys a specific event. Time yourself while reading the scene aloud. Now, rewrite the scene, adjusting it to be either faster-paced or slower-paced, and time yourself again. Discuss how the changes affected the way you read the scene and how it might affect the audience's experience.

4. **Pacing Peer Review:** Share a scene you've written with a classmate and discuss its pacing. Offer suggestions on how to adjust the pace if needed. Do the same for their scene, providing constructive feedback.

5. **Storyboard and Pacing:** Create a storyboard for a short animation sequence. Consider how the flow of images and transitions can contribute to the overall pace of your story.

Chapter 16: Subplots and Parallel Storylines: Expanding Your Narrative Universe

Stories don't exist in a vacuum. A well-crafted narrative can be enriched by the addition of subplots and parallel storylines. This chapter explores how to integrate these elements effectively, weaving them into the main plot without overwhelming your audience.

16.1 The Power of Subplots

A subplot is a secondary story that runs alongside the main plot. Subplots can offer several advantages:

- **Character Development:** Subplots can explore side characters' motivations and experiences, adding depth and richness to the overall story.

- **World-Building:** Subplots can introduce details about the setting and history of your world, giving it a more lived-in feel.

- **Raising Stakes:** Subplots can build tension or create complications that impact the main plot, increasing the overall stakes for your characters.

- **Creating Contrast:** Subplots can offer a change of pace or tone compared to the main plot, keeping the audience engaged and preventing monotony.

  However, subplots can backfire if not managed well. Here's how to integrate them effectively:

- **Keep it Connected:** Subplots should be relevant to the main plot in some way. They can connect thematically, reveal hidden information, or offer character development that impacts the main narrative.

- **Focus and Balance:** Don't introduce too many subplots. Each subplot should be well-developed enough to be engaging while ensuring the main plot remains the central focus.

- **Resolution:** Just like the main plot, subplots need satisfying resolutions that tie up loose ends.

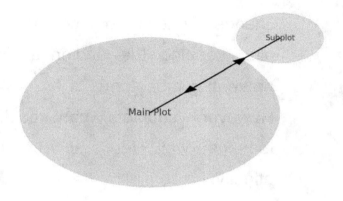

Image: A visual representation of a story with a main plot and a subplot. An imaginary diagram with two circles, one larger representing the main plot.

16.2 Parallel Storylines: A Balancing Act

Parallel storylines are separate narratives that run concurrently with the main plot. These can be particularly effective in certain genres like science fiction or fantasy. However, managing parallel storylines requires even greater skill:

- **Clearly Defined Storylines:** Each parallel storyline needs a distinct purpose and clear goals for its characters.

- **Crossover Potential:** Consider ways for the separate storylines to intersect or influence each other at key moments, heightening the impact of both.

- **Maintaining Coherence:** With multiple storylines, it's crucial to ensure a smooth flow and avoid confusing the audience. Utilize clear transitions and pacing to keep the story clear.

16.3 Case Study: Subplots and Parallel Stories in Action - "Avatar: The Last Airbender"

"Avatar: The Last Airbender" is a prime example of effective subplot and parallel storyline usage. Aang's quest to master the elements (main plot) is complemented by subplots focusing on Zuko's internal conflict and redemption arc. Additionally, the show weaves in parallel storylines like Iroh's capture and the ongoing war, all intertwining to create a rich and engaging narrative tapestry.

Image: Poster of Avatar: The Last Airbender.
Courtesy: Pinterest

16.4 Review Questions

1. Explain what a subplot is and how it can enhance your storytelling.
2. Discuss the different benefits of using subplots.
3. How can you ensure subplots are well-integrated and don't detract from the main plot?
4. What are the challenges of using parallel storylines? How can you overcome them?
5. Analyze how "Avatar: The Last Airbender" utilizes subplots and parallel storylines to enrich its narrative.

16.5 Suggested Practical Exercises

1. **Identifying Subplots:** Choose an animated film or series and analyze its use of subplots. Identify the subplots, discuss their connection to the main plot, and explain how they enhance the story.

2. **Developing a Subplot:** Create a subplot for a story you're working on. Consider how this subplot will connect to the main plot, develop the characters involved, or build the world you've created.

3. **Parallel Storyline Brainstorming:** Develop a concept for an animated project that utilizes parallel storylines. Discuss the potential connections and interactions between these storylines and how they will ultimately converge.

4. **Storyboard Collaboration:** Work with a classmate to create a storyboard sequence that depicts the intersection of two storylines. Discuss how the visuals will help communicate the flow and relationship between these narratives.

5. **Peer Review:** Share your subplot or parallel storyline ideas with a classmate and offer constructive feedback. Do the same for their ideas, helping them refine their approach.

Chapter 17: Plot Devices and Twists: Adding Surprise and Sizzle to Your Story

A good plot keeps the audience on their toes. This chapter explores common plot devices and how to craft effective plot twists that surprise and engage viewers.

17.1 The Toolbox of Plot Devices

Plot devices are narrative elements that can be used to advance the story, create suspense, or deepen character development. Here are some common ones:

- **MacGuffin:** This is an object or goal that drives the plot forward, even if its intrinsic value is not particularly important. For example, in "Raiders of the Lost Ark," the Ark of the Covenant is a MacGuffin that motivates characters but doesn't hold any specific significance within the story itself.

- **Foreshadowing:** Subtly hinting at future events can build anticipation and reward attentive viewers. This can be done through dialogue, imagery, or symbolism.

- **Flashback:** A flashback takes the audience back in time, revealing past events that influence the present. This can be used for character development, explanation, or building suspense.

- **Cliffhanger:** An ending scene that leaves the audience with a burning question or unresolved conflict, creating a desire to see what happens next.

- **Red Herring:** This is a misleading clue or event that intentionally throws the audience off track, keeping the story unpredictable.

Image: An illustration that depicts storytelling tools symbolically. A quill and ink bottle to symbolize writing and narrative voice, A compass for guiding the plot or structure of a story, A theater mask to represent character development, A book to symbolize the overall story or plot, A candle to represent themes or the mood of the story, and A clock for time-related elements like flashbacks or pacing.

Using Plot Devices Effectively:

While plot devices can be helpful, overuse can feel cheap or manipulative. Use them strategically to enhance your story, not as a crutch:

- **Justify their presence:** Ensure each plot device is logically connected to your story's world and characters.

- **Maintain consistency:** Don't introduce new elements that contradict previously established rules of your world.

- **Balance surprise with foreshadowing:** While plot twists should be surprising, some foreshadowing allows the audience to feel engaged and rewarded for picking up on clues.

17.2 The Art of the Plot Twist

A well-executed plot twist can be a powerful tool for surprising and engaging your audience. Here are some tips for crafting effective twists:

- **Subvert expectations:** Don't be predictable. Take established ideas or seemingly harmless information and turn them on their head.
- **Plant the seeds:** Subtly foreshadow the twist throughout the story, dropping hints that can be reinterpreted upon revelation.
- **High Stakes:** The consequences of the twist should be significant, raising the stakes for the characters and increasing audience engagement.
- **Emotional Impact:** Aim for twists that not only surprise but also evoke strong emotions in the audience.

Remember: Don't twist for the sake of twisting. Ensure the twist organically stems from your narrative and enhances the overall story.

17.3 Case Study: A Masterclass in Twists - "The Sixth Sense"

M. Night Shyamalan's "The Sixth Sense" is a classic example of a film built on a powerful plot twist. The film cleverly creates a sense of mystery while subtly planting clues that point to the shocking revelation at the end. The twist doesn't feel random but emerges organically from the story and character development, making it a truly impactful moment.

Image: Poster of The Sixth sense. Courtesy: IMDb.com

17.4 Review Questions

1. Define a plot device and explain how it can be used to enhance your story.
2. Discuss different kinds of plot devices and their potential applications.
3. How can you ensure plot devices are used strategically and don't detract from the overall story?
4. What are the key ingredients for crafting an effective plot twist?
5. Analyze how "The Sixth Sense" uses foreshadowing and surprise to create a powerful plot twist.

17.5 Suggested Practical Exercises

1. **Identifying Plot Devices:** Watch an animated film or series and identify instances of plot devices being used. Discuss how these devices advance the story, build suspense, or develop characters.
2. **Reimagining a Story with Plot Devices:** Choose a familiar story and discuss how you

could incorporate different plot devices to create a fresh perspective.

3. **Surprise Ending Brainstorming:** Develop a story with a surprise ending. Consider how you can subtly foreshadow the twist throughout the story without giving it away too soon.

4. **Twist Rewrite:** Rewrite the climax of a story, incorporating a surprising plot twist. Analyze how the twist changes the audience's perception of the story and its characters.

5. **Peer Review:** Share your plot twist idea or a story rewrite with a classmate and discuss its effectiveness.

Chapter 18: Workshop: Building Your Animated Story

This chapter serves as your personal animation storytelling laboratory! It's time to take the concepts explored in this section and apply them to your own animated project. We'll guide you through developing and outlining a compelling plot for your class project.

18.1 Brainstorming Bonanza!

Before diving into specifics, unleash your creativity! Brainstorm ideas for your animated project. Here are some prompts to get your juices flowing:

- **Genre Exploration:** Do you have a favorite genre (comedy, sci-fi, fantasy)? Consider a twist on it or explore a genre mashup.
- **Character Inspiration:** Have you encountered a fictional character or real-life

person you find fascinating? Design a story
around them.

- **Thematic Focus:** What message or feeling
  do you want to evoke in your audience? Craft
  a story that tackles that theme.
- **Concept Fusion:** Combine two seemingly
  unrelated ideas and explore the possibilities.

Image: A team conducting a brainstorming session.

Once you have a general direction, narrow down your ideas and start fleshing out a central conflict.

18.2 Crafting Your Core Conflict

A strong conflict forms the backbone of your story. What is your protagonist's goal? What obstacles stand in their way? Explore different conflict types:

- **Internal Conflict:** Your character struggles with their own emotions, beliefs, or desires.
- **External Conflict:** Your character faces a villain, force of nature, or societal issue.

Here are some brainstorming tools:

- **Character Profiles:** Create profiles for your main characters, outlining their goals, motivations, and weaknesses.
- **Conflict Charts:** Draw a chart with your protagonist on one side and their antagonists on the other. Brainstorm potential challenges and obstacles each side might encounter.

18.3 Building the Plot Outline

With your conflict established, it's time to outline your plot. This provides a roadmap for your story, ensuring a logical flow and satisfying resolution. Here's a common three-act structure to consider:

Act 1: Introduction (Exposition & Setup)

- Introduce the main characters and setting.
- Establish the central conflict and protagonist's goal.
- Introduce the antagonist or opposing force.

Act 2: Rising Action & Challenges

- Raise the stakes for your protagonist.
- Present escalating challenges that test their resolve.
- Allow for character development and growth.

Act 3: Climax, Resolution, & Denouement

- The protagonist faces their biggest challenge in the climax.
- The conflict is resolved, either through success or failure.
- Tie up loose ends and provide closure for the audience.

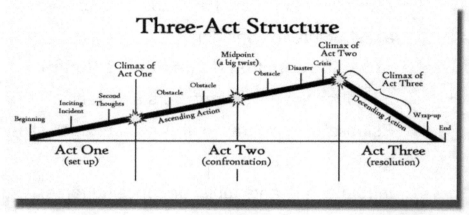

Image: A visual representation of the three-act structure.

Remember, this is a flexible framework. Some stories might benefit from a different structure. Here are some resources to help you build your plot outline:

- **Storyboarding Software:** Use storyboarding software to visually map out your plot points.

- **Plot Point Outlining Templates:** Find templates online that guide you through key plot points in each act.

18.4 Case Study: From Outline to Animation - "Zootopia"

Disney's "Zootopia" demonstrates a well-structured plot. The film starts with Judy Hopps' dream of becoming a police officer in a city divided by species. (Act 1) As she faces discrimination and prejudice, the stakes rise as she stumbles upon a conspiracy. (Act 2) The film builds to a thrilling climax where Judy exposes the truth and earns the respect of her peers. (Act 3) This story effectively utilizes the three-act structure to create a compelling and satisfying narrative.

Image: Poster of Zootopia. Courtesy: Disney

18.5 Review Questions

1. Why is brainstorming important in the story development process?
2. Differentiate between internal and external conflict. How can these be combined for a richer story?
3. Explain the three-act structure and how it can be used to create a satisfying plot outline.
4. Discuss different tools and resources available to help you build your plot outline.
5. Analyze how "Zootopia" utilizes the three-act structure to tell a compelling story.

18.6 Suggested Practical Exercises

1. **Story Brainstorming:** Spend 10 minutes brainstorming potential story ideas. Use brainstorming prompts provided or come up with your own. Choose your favorite concept and jot down a brief synopsis

Story

Module III: Plot and Structure

Story Title: "The Clockmaker's Secret"

Story Concept:

This story will highlight the importance of plot and structure, illustrating how a well-organized sequence of events, with clear exposition, rising action, climax, falling action, and resolution, can create a compelling narrative.

The Clockmaker's Secret

In the bustling city of Pendulum, time was everything. The city was famous for its intricate clocks, each crafted by the master clockmaker, Mr. Horace. His clocks were not just timepieces; they were masterpieces, renowned for their precision and beauty. Yet, despite his success, Mr. Horace was a reclusive man, seldom seen outside his workshop. Rumors swirled around the city about the secret behind his remarkable clocks.

One day, a young apprentice named Leo arrived at Mr. Horace's workshop, eager to learn the art of clockmaking. Leo had heard the rumors and was determined to uncover the clockmaker's secret. Mr. Horace agreed to take him on, but with a stern warning: "Patience and discipline are the keys to mastering this craft. If you seek shortcuts, you will only find failure."

Leo began his apprenticeship with enthusiasm, but as the days turned into weeks, he grew frustrated. Mr. Horace was a strict teacher, and the work was tedious. Leo longed to discover the secret of the clocks, but Mr. Horace never spoke of it, focusing only on the basics of the craft.

One night, after Mr. Horace had retired to his chambers, Leo decided to explore the workshop. He searched through drawers, examined old blueprints, and tinkered with unfinished clocks, but found nothing unusual. Then, behind a dusty curtain, he discovered a locked door. Convinced that the secret was hidden behind it, Leo tried to pick the lock, but it was too intricate.

Frustrated, Leo decided to confront Mr. Horace the next morning. When he did, Mr. Horace was not angry, but he was disappointed. "You lack the patience to see the truth," he said. "The secret you seek cannot be found through force."

Over the next few months, Leo refocused on his training. He learned the intricacies of gears and springs, the importance of precision, and the beauty of balance in design. Slowly, he began to understand the craft on a deeper level. The clocks he made became more refined, and he earned Mr. Horace's respect.

One day, Mr. Horace took Leo to the locked door. "You have earned the right to see what lies beyond," he said, handing Leo a key. Inside, the room was filled with the most magnificent clocks Leo had ever seen. But there was something different about these clocks—they didn't just measure time; they controlled it.

Mr. Horace revealed that these clocks were enchanted, capable of altering the flow of time within the city. He had created them with the intention of helping the people of Pendulum, but he had realized that such power could easily be misused. The secret of the clocks was not in their mechanics, but in the responsibility that came with controlling time itself.

Mr. Horace entrusted Leo with the knowledge, but with a final lesson: "The structure of time, like the structure of a story, must be respected. A story without structure is chaos, just as time without order is disaster."

Leo spent the rest of his days as a clockmaker in Pendulum, continuing the work of his master. He understood now that the true secret of the clocks was not in their enchantment, but in the discipline, patience, and respect for the craft. And just as a clock must be meticulously constructed to keep time, a story must be carefully structured to captivate its audience.

Analysis: This story illustrates the essential elements of plot and structure, with a clear exposition (introduction of Leo and the city of Pendulum), rising action (Leo's growing frustration and discovery of the locked door), climax (the revelation of the enchanted clocks), falling action (Mr. Horace's explanation), and resolution (Leo's acceptance of his role as the new clockmaker). The narrative structure mirrors the lessons within the story, showing how important it is to respect the structure of both time and storytelling.

Module IV
Writing for Multimedia

Chapter 19: Writing for Animation: Bringing Your Characters to Life

Animation offers a unique storytelling medium, allowing for boundless creativity and visual splendor. But how does the writing process differ from crafting a script for live-action? This chapter delves into the techniques and considerations specific to writing for animation.

19.1 Animation Script Essentials

While animation scripts share similarities with their live-action counterparts, they emphasize certain aspects:

- **Visual Specificity:** Animation scripts go beyond describing actions. They provide detailed descriptions of visuals, including character movements, expressions, and camera angles.

- **Economy of Words:** Since animation is a visual medium, dialogue needs to be concise and impactful.
- **Action and Emotion:** Animation scripts should convey character actions and emotions clearly, as these will be primarily communicated through visuals.

Here's a breakdown of key elements in an animation script:

- **Slugline:** This identifies the scene location and time (e.g., INT. SPACESHIP - DAY).
- **Action Lines:** These describe what's happening visually, including character movements, expressions, and background details.
- **Dialogue:** This is the spoken conversation between characters. Keep it focused and avoid lengthy monologues.
- **Parentheticals:** These offer additional information about character emotions, vocal delivery, or sound effects.

- **Transitions:** These provide instructions for scene changes (e.g., FADE OUT, CUT TO BLACK).

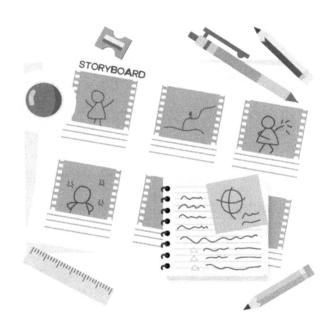

Image: illustration of a sample animation script page. Courtesy: Pngtree.com

Remember: Formatting can vary depending on the studio, but understanding these core elements will serve as a strong foundation.

19.2 Beyond Live-Action: Embracing Animation's Strengths

Writing for animation unlocks unique storytelling possibilities. Unlike live-action, animation is not limited by physical constraints or special effects budgets. Here's how to leverage animation's strengths:

- **Visual Storytelling:** Embrace the power of visuals! Utilize action, expressions, and character design to convey emotions and story elements.

- **World-Building:** Design vibrant and imaginative settings that wouldn't be possible in live-action. Animation allows for boundless creativity in world-building.

- **Stylistic Exploration:** Animation can seamlessly blend different art styles and techniques. Experiment and find a visual style that complements your story.

- **Humor and Timing:** Animation excels at physical humor and exaggerated expressions. Utilize timing and visual gags to create comedic moments.

19.3 Case Study: A Masterclass in Animation Scriptwriting - "Gravity Falls"

"Gravity Falls" by Alex Hirsch exemplifies the strengths of animation scripting. The show utilizes concise dialogue, detailed action lines to convey character emotions, and vibrant visuals that seamlessly blend humor and mystery. The script embraces the fantastical setting, creating a world that wouldn't be possible in live-action.

Image: Poster of Gravity Falls. Courtesy: The Hollywood Reporter

19.4 Review Questions

1. Explain the key differences between writing for animation and live-action.

2. Discuss the importance of visual specificity in animation scripts.

3. How can animation scripts effectively convey character emotions and actions using minimal dialogue?

4. What are some unique storytelling advantages offered by animation?

5. Analyze how "Gravity Falls" utilizes animation scriptwriting techniques to create a compelling and visually engaging narrative.

19.5 Suggested Practical Exercises

1. **Animation Script Analysis:** Choose a scene from an animated film or series and analyze its script. Discuss how visual details, action lines, and dialogue work together to tell the story.

2. **Script Adaptation:** Choose a scene from a live-action film and rewrite it as an animation script. Consider how you can use animation's strengths to enhance the storytelling.

3. **World-Building through Scripting:** Develop a unique setting for an animated short film. Write a short scene that showcases this world through visual descriptions and character actions in an animation script format.

4. **Action & Emotion Exercise:** Write a short animation scene that conveys a specific emotion (e.g., fear, joy, surprise) through

character actions and expressions only, with minimal dialogue.

5. **Peer Review:** Share your animation script excerpt or scene concept with a classmate and discuss its effectiveness. Offer feedback on their work as well.

Chapter 20: Interactive Storytelling: Empowering Your Audience

Welcome to the realm of interactive storytelling! Unlike traditional narratives, here, the audience actively participates, shaping the story's direction and influencing the outcome. This chapter explores the principles of interactive narratives and how to write for video games and other interactive media.

20.1 Branching Narratives and Player Choice

Interactive narratives break free from a linear path. Players make choices throughout the story that impact the characters, the plot, and even the ending. This branching structure encourages replayability and a sense of agency for the audience.

- **Choice Points:** These are moments where players are presented with options that influence the story's progression. These choices can be simple or complex, with far-reaching consequences.

- **World Building for Exploration:** Interactive narratives often have expansive worlds filled with secrets and side quests. Writing for these worlds involves creating a sense of discovery and rewarding players for exploration.

- **Character Development with Player Input:** Player choices can shape a character's personality, relationships, and even morality. Consider writing characters who are adaptable and react dynamically to player decisions.

[Illustration Option]: A branching narrative diagram could be included here. Imagine a tree with a thick trunk representing the story's beginning. As the branches split, each represents a different choice a player can make, leading to different storylines or destinations.

20.2 Writing for Video Games: A Multifaceted Approach

Video games are a prime example of interactive storytelling. Here are key aspects to consider when writing for this medium:

- **Balancing Narrative and Gameplay:** While story is important, compelling gameplay mechanics are equally crucial. Strike a balance between engaging narrative and engaging gameplay.

- **Character Dialogue and Voice Acting:** Video game characters need realistic and engaging dialogue that reflects their personalities and reactions to player choices. Consider how voice acting can further enhance these interactions.

- **World-Building Through Exploration and Lore:** Players actively explore the game world. Create a captivating environment with hidden details, lore entries, and environmental storytelling to enrich the narrative.

- **Quest Design: Meaningful Choices with Consequences:** Structure quests in a way that presents meaningful choices with clear consequences. This encourages players to consider the impact of their actions.

Remember: Writing for interactive media requires collaboration. Work closely with game designers and programmers to ensure a seamless integration of story and gameplay.

20.3 Case Study: A Masterclass in Interactive Storytelling - "Life is Strange"

"Life is Strange" is a game that exemplifies the power of interactive storytelling. Players control Max Caulfield, a teenager who discovers she can rewind time. Through her choices, players navigate complex relationships, influence the fate of characters, and ultimately shape the story's conclusion. "Life is Strange" demonstrates how effective use of branching narratives, character development, and player agency can create a deeply engaging and impactful experience.

Image: Poster of Life is Strange game.

Courtesy: Playstation.com

20.4 Review Questions

1. Explain the concept of interactive storytelling and how it differs from traditional narratives.
2. Describe the role of player choice in interactive narratives. How can writers incorporate choice with meaningful consequences?
3. Discuss the importance of world-building in interactive media. How can writing contribute to a sense of discovery and exploration?
4. What are some key considerations when writing for video games? How do you balance narrative with gameplay mechanics?
5. Analyze how "Life is Strange" utilizes interactive storytelling techniques to create a compelling and engaging experience.

20.5 Suggested Practical Exercises

1. **Interactive Story Brainstorming:** Come up with a story concept that could be adapted into an interactive format. Discuss potential choice points and how player decisions might influence the narrative.

2. **Dialogue for Choice:** Write a sample dialogue scene with multiple branching options based on player choices. Consider how the character's responses and the story's direction might change depending on the chosen path.

3. **World-Building for Exploration:** Design a small section of a game world, focusing on environmental details and hidden clues that can be discovered by players. Describe this section in a way that evokes a sense of mystery and encourages further exploration.

4. **Interactive Prototype Creation:** Utilize online tools or basic coding to create a simple, interactive story prototype with branching narratives. Focus on a single choice point and its immediate consequences.

5. **Peer Review:** Share your interactive story concept, dialogue scene, or world-building description with a classmate and discuss its

effectiveness. Provide feedback on their work as well.

Chapter 21: Transmedia Storytelling: Weaving Narratives Across Platforms

Imagine a story that transcends the confines of a single medium. Transmedia storytelling utilizes multiple platforms, each offering unique pieces of the narrative puzzle. This chapter explores the exciting world of transmedia storytelling, discussing its potential and the challenges it presents.

21.1 A World Unbound: The Power of Transmedia

Transmedia narratives unfold across various platforms, including:

- **Animation and Film:** This can be the core narrative experience, with additional content offered through other media.

- **Video Games:** Interactive elements and deeper exploration of the world can be offered through games.

- **Websites and Apps:** These can provide backstory, character profiles, or interactive experiences to expand the world.
- **Social Media:** Engaging with audiences and fostering a sense of community can be achieved through social media platforms.

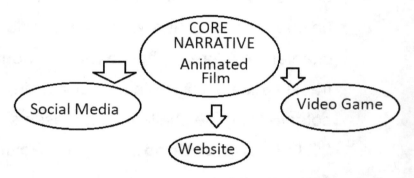

Image: A visual representation of transmedia storytelling: A central circle labeled "Core Narrative" (e.g., Animated Film). Around this circle, smaller circles branch out, representing different platforms (Video Game, Website, Social Media) with arrows showing how they connect and expand the core narrative.

Benefits of Transmedia Storytelling:

- **Deeper Audience Engagement:** By offering content across platforms, transmedia narratives keep audiences engaged and actively seeking out new pieces of the story.

- **World-Building on a Grand Scale:** The story's universe can be explored in much greater detail across various mediums, creating a richer and more immersive experience.

- **Multi-Perspective Storytelling:** Different platforms can offer unique viewpoints on characters and events, enriching the overall narrative.

21.2 Challenges and Strategies for the Transmedia Trailblazer

Crafting a compelling transmedia narrative requires careful planning and consideration:

- **Maintaining Cohesion:** While stories unfold across platforms, they should feel interconnected and part of a unified whole. A well-defined core narrative provides a foundation.

- **Content Accessibility:** Ensure each platform offers a satisfying experience, even for audiences who haven't engaged with the story on every platform.
- **Audience Participation:** Transmedia narratives often encourage audience participation. Plan for how to integrate and manage audience contributions effectively.

Strategies for Success:

- **Develop a Transmedia Bible:** This document outlines the story's core elements, world-building details, and how each platform will contribute to the narrative.
- **Collaboration is Key:** Transmedia projects often involve teams with expertise in different media formats. Effective communication and collaboration are crucial.

- **Start Small, Scale Up:** Don't be overwhelmed! Begin with a core narrative and expand across platforms as your project evolves.

21.3 Case Study: A Transmedia Masterpiece - "The ARG of Why So Serious?"

The viral marketing campaign for "The Dark Knight" film exemplifies a successful transmedia experience. An Alternate Reality Game (ARG) titled "Why So Serious?" unfolded online and in real-world locations. Players deciphered clues, solved puzzles, and interacted with characters, all to unravel a mystery connected to the film's plot. This transmedia campaign effectively generated excitement and anticipation for the film, blurring the lines between reality and fiction.

Image: Poster of Why So Serious? Courtesy: Tumblr.com

21.4 Review Questions

1. Explain the concept of transmedia storytelling and how it differs from traditional storytelling methods.

2. Discuss the potential benefits of transmedia narratives for both creators and audiences.

3. Identify some challenges associated with transmedia storytelling. How can these challenges be overcome?

4. What are some strategies for developing and launching a successful transmedia project?

5. Analyze how the "Why So Serious?" ARG campaign utilized transmedia principles to create an engaging and immersive experience for audiences.

21.5 Suggested Practical Exercises

1. **Transmedia Brainstorming:** Choose a story concept and brainstorm how it could be adapted into a transmedia experience. Consider what content would be offered on different platforms and how audiences would interact with the story across these platforms.

2. **Developing a Transmedia Bible:** Create a basic outline for a transmedia story, focusing on the core narrative, world-building details, and potential content for different platforms (e.g., animation, website, social media).

3. **Design a Transmedia Puzzle:** Develop a puzzle or interactive element that could be used in a transmedia narrative. Consider how

this puzzle would fit into the story and how audiences would solve it.

4. **Research and Analysis:** Research a successful transmedia project and analyze how it utilizes different platforms to tell its story. Discuss the project's strengths and potential areas for improvement.

5. **Peer Collaboration:** Team up with classmates and brainstorm a transmedia concept together. Discuss

Chapter 22: Writing for the Digital Age: Captivating Audiences Online

The digital landscape offers a vibrant platform for storytelling. This chapter explores the art of crafting compelling narratives for web series, short films, and online content. We'll discuss how to adapt traditional writing techniques to engage audiences thriving in the digital world.

22.1 The Digital Stage: Short Attention Spans, High Expectations

The digital world presents both opportunities and challenges for writers. Audiences have shorter attention spans and are bombarded with content. Here's how to adjust your writing for online success:

- **Strong Hook and Engaging Pacing:** Hook viewers quickly with a captivating opening and maintain a fast-paced narrative that keeps them scrolling or watching.

- **Conciseness and Clarity:** Writing for online content requires conciseness and clarity. Ensure your message is clear and impactful, avoiding unnecessary wordiness.

- **Visually Appealing Storytelling:** Maximize the visual aspect of your narrative. Utilize descriptive language and consider how visuals (e.g., animation, graphics) can enhance your story.

Image: A surfer riding a wave with a laptop screen replacing: "Catching the digital wave: Engaging online audiences." Courtesy: Behance.net

Additional Considerations for Different Formats:

- **Web Series:** Break down stories into bite-sized episodes perfect for binge-watching. Emphasize cliffhangers and serialized elements to keep viewers coming back for more.

- **Short Films:** Focus on a tightly structured narrative with a clear conflict and resolution. Utilize the short format to deliver a powerful emotional impact or thought-provoking message.

- **Online Content:** Tailor your writing style to the specific platform (e.g., social media, blog). Utilize keywords and optimize content for searchability.

22.2 Adapting the Classics: Traditional Techniques for Modern Audiences

While the digital landscape presents unique challenges, the core principles of storytelling remain the same. Here's how to adapt traditional writing techniques for the online world:

- **Character Development:** Create relatable and engaging characters even within short online formats. Focus on showcasing their desires and conflicts in a dynamic way.

- **Conflict and Stakes:** Every story needs a conflict that drives the narrative forward. Raise the stakes for your characters in the digital world to keep viewers invested.

- **Dialogue:** Write realistic dialogue that sounds natural and fits the characters' personalities. While conciseness is key, allow for character development through dialogue.

Remember: Effective storytelling is about connecting with your audience. While keeping the digital world's fast pace in mind, don't sacrifice the depth and emotional resonance of your narrative.

22.3 Case Study: Storytelling Success - "The Lizzie Bennet Diaries"

"The Lizzie Bennet Diaries" is a prime example of adapting a classic story for the digital age. This web series retells Jane Austen's "Pride and Prejudice" through the lens of video blogs, drawing in a new generation of audiences. The series effectively uses humor, relatable characters, and a visually engaging format to capture the essence of the original story while remaining fresh and innovative.

Image: Poster of The Lizzie Bennet Diaries

Courtesy: Nerds and Beyond.com

22.4 Review Questions

1. Discuss the unique challenges and opportunities presented by writing for a digital audience.

2. How can writers captivate online audiences with short attention spans?

3. Explain how writing for web series, short films, and online content might differ in approach.

4. How can we adapt traditional writing techniques like character development and conflict to the digital format?

5. Analyze how "The Lizzie Bennet Diaries" successfully utilized an online format to tell a classic story in a way that resonates with a modern audience.

22.5 Suggested Practical Exercises

1. **Digital Story Brainstorming:** Come up with a story concept specifically tailored for a digital platform (e.g., web series, Instagram story).

Consider how the format would influence the narrative structure and pacing.

2. **Adapting a Classic:** Choose a classic short story and rewrite it as a script for a short online film. Identify specific changes you made to adapt the story for a digital audience.

3. **Dialogue for Online Engagement:** Write a short dialogue scene for a web series episode. Focus on creating natural, engaging dialogue that reflects the characters' personalities and propels the story forward.

4. **Script Breakdown and Analysis:** Analyze a script from a successful web series or short online film. Discuss how the writers utilize pacing, cliffhangers, and visual elements to engage audiences.

5. **Peer Review:** Share your digital story concept, script excerpt, or online content idea with a classmate and discuss its effectiveness in capturing a digital audience's attention.

Chapter 23: Visual Storytelling: The Power of the Image

The human brain processes visuals much faster than text. In multimedia storytelling, visuals take center stage, captivating audiences and enriching narratives. This chapter explores the importance of visuals in multimedia and how to integrate them seamlessly with your writing.

23.1 Beyond Words: The Magic of Visual Storytelling

Visuals are a powerful storytelling tool. They can:

- **Convey Emotion Instantly:** A well-chosen image or animation can evoke a range of emotions in viewers quicker and more effectively than words alone.

- **World-Building and Setting the Scene:** Visuals establish the setting, immersing audiences in the story's world. A detailed background or a character design can communicate volumes about the environment and characters.

- **Driving the Narrative Forward:** Visuals can be used to advance the plot without relying solely on dialogue. Action sequences, character interactions, and even subtle expressions can move the story forward.

A brave adventurer fighting a ferocious dragon with a fiery sword.

Image: A comparison image. On one side, a scene described solely with text. On the other side, the same scene with a captivating image.

Remember: Visuals are not mere decoration; they are an integral part of the storytelling process.

23.2 The Art of Integration: Text and Visuals Working Together

Effective multimedia storytelling requires a seamless blend of text and visuals. Here are some key strategies:

- **Clarity and Purpose:** Every visual element should have a clear purpose in the narrative. Avoid cluttering your story with unnecessary images or graphics.

- **Complementary Storytelling:** Text and visuals should complement each other. Don't repeat the same information; let them work together to paint a richer picture.

- **Visual Hierarchy:** Guide the viewer's eye. Use size, color, and placement to prioritize important visual elements and direct attention to key information.

Additional Considerations:

- **Animation and Motion Graphics:** In animation and multimedia projects, movement and dynamic visuals can further enhance storytelling.
- **Cinematography and Camera Angles:** For video-based multimedia, consider how camera angles and shot composition can add depth and meaning to the narrative.

23.3 Case Study: A Masterclass in Visual Storytelling - "Spirited Away"

Hayao Miyazaki's "Spirited Away" is a compelling example of visual storytelling. The film utilizes stunning animation, breathtaking landscapes, and expressive character designs to create a magical and immersive world. The visuals seamlessly complement the narrative, conveying emotions, establishing the setting, and driving the story forward.

[Illustration Option]: Here, you could include a screenshot from "Spirited Away" that showcases the film's use of captivating visuals to tell the story.

23.4 Review Questions

1. Explain the importance of visuals in multimedia storytelling. How do visuals enhance narratives compared to text alone?

2. Discuss different ways visuals can be used to convey emotions, establish setting, and advance the plot.

3. How can writers ensure a seamless integration of text and visuals in their multimedia projects?

4. What additional considerations are there for using animation, motion graphics, and cinematography to enhance visual storytelling?

5. Analyze how "Spirited Away" utilizes visuals to create a captivating and immersive experience for the audience.

23.5 Suggested Practical Exercises

1. **Visual Storytelling Brainstorming:** Choose a scene from a story and brainstorm how

visuals (images, animations, graphics) could be used to tell that scene effectively. Consider what emotions you want to evoke and how visuals can enhance the message.

2. **Script with Visual Integration:** Write a short scene for a multimedia project, incorporating visuals into your script. Describe the visuals and how they will work with the dialogue and narrative flow.

3. **Image Analysis:** Analyze a scene from a multimedia project (animation, video game, website). Discuss how visuals are used to tell the story, considering aspects like composition, color, and symbolism.

4. **Storyboard Creation:** Develop a storyboard for a short animation sequence. Use sketches or basic visuals to depict key moments in the narrative and plan how visuals will be used to tell the story.

5. **Peer Review:** Share your visual storytelling brainstorm, script with visuals, or image

analysis with a classmate and discuss the effectiveness of your approach.

Chapter 24: Writing for Multimedia: Case Study

In this chapter, we'll delve deeper into the world of multimedia storytelling by analyzing successful projects. By dissecting what makes these narratives work, we can gain valuable insights and apply them to our own writing endeavors.

Analysis of Successful Multimedia Storytelling Projects

The beauty of multimedia storytelling lies in its ability to weave together narrative threads using various media. Let's explore a few examples:

- **Interactive Documentary:** Imagine a documentary film where viewers can click on elements within the video, leading them to additional information, interviews, or historical photographs. This interactivity keeps the audience engaged and allows them to delve deeper into specific aspects of the story.

Illustration Opportunity: Here, you could include a screenshot or mockup of an interactive documentary interface.

- **Augmented Reality (AR) Experience:** AR merges the real world with virtual elements. Imagine an AR app that allows users to explore a historical city by holding their phone up to specific landmarks. They might see a 3D recreation of the landmark in its former glory, accompanied by audio narration or historical text.

- **Animated Explainers:** Complex concepts can be made engaging and accessible through animation. Explainer videos often employ humor, visual metaphors, and clear narration to deliver information in a concise and memorable way.

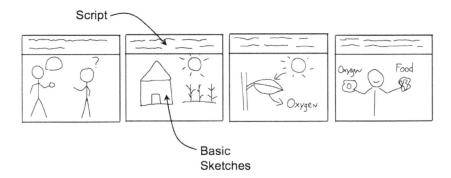

Image: A storyboard panel from an explainer video, showcasing the use of visuals and text.

These are just a few examples, and the possibilities are endless. But what are the key ingredients that make these projects successful?

Here are some elements to consider:

- **Strong Narrative Core:** There needs to be a compelling story at the heart of the project. Whether it's historical, biographical, or fictional, the story should draw viewers in and make them care about the characters and events.

- **Effective Use of Multimedia:** The multimedia elements should complement and enhance the narrative, not overwhelm it. Each element, be it video, animation, audio, or text, should serve a specific purpose and contribute to the overall story.

- **Target Audience:** Understanding your audience is crucial. The writing style, visuals, and level of interactivity should be tailored to resonate with your intended viewers.

- **User Experience (UX) Design:** Consider how users will navigate and interact with your multimedia piece. The interface should be user-friendly and intuitive, allowing viewers to experience the story seamlessly.

By analyzing successful projects, we can learn valuable lessons about structuring narratives, integrating multimedia elements, and engaging audiences. Now, let's test our understanding with a real-world example!

Case Study: Project X (Choose a specific multimedia project and analyze it based on the points mentioned previously)

Here's where you come in! Choose a specific and well-known multimedia project, such as an interactive documentary, an AR app, or a popular animated explainer video. Briefly describe the project, then analyze its storytelling elements:

- What is the core narrative?
- How does the project use multimedia effectively?
- Who is the target audience?
- How does the project create a user-friendly experience?

By dissecting a real-world case study, you'll gain a deeper understanding of storytelling principles and their application in multimedia projects.

Review Questions

- What are some of the advantages of multimedia storytelling?
- How can you analyze the effectiveness of a multimedia project?
- Consider a multimedia project you've enjoyed – what elements made it successful?
- What are some of the challenges associated with writing for multimedia platforms?

Suggested Practical Exercises

- Choose a historical event or scientific concept and brainstorm ways to create an interactive multimedia presentation about it.
- Write a script for a short animated explainer video on a topic of your choice.
- Develop a storyboard for an AR experience that showcases a specific location or event. By engaging in these exercises, you'll put your storytelling skills into practice and gain valuable experience in writing for multimedia platforms. Through analysis and practice,

you'll be well on your way to crafting engaging and impactful multimedia stories!

Module IV: Writing for Multimedia

Story Title: "Echoes of the Forgotten Realm"

Story Concept:

This story will showcase the unique challenges and opportunities in writing for multimedia, such as incorporating interactive elements, multiple perspectives, and non-linear storytelling.

Echoes of the Forgotten Realm

In a future not too distant from our own, the line between the physical and digital worlds had blurred. People could now immerse themselves in virtual realms, experiencing adventures, solving mysteries, and interacting with others in ways once unimaginable. One of the most popular virtual worlds was the Forgotten Realm, a mysterious and ever-changing landscape filled with ancient ruins, hidden secrets, and powerful artifacts.

The story follows three main characters, each with a different role in the Forgotten Realm:

1. **Ava**, a skilled explorer who specializes in uncovering hidden treasures and ancient knowledge.

2. **Liam**, a hacker with the ability to manipulate the code of the virtual world, creating shortcuts, altering environments, and accessing forbidden areas.

3. **Nia**, a historian who has dedicated her life to understanding the origins and history of the Forgotten Realm, seeking the truth behind its creation.

Each character's journey is intertwined, yet their experiences within the Forgotten Realm are unique and shaped by their individual skills and choices.

Chapter 1: The Arrival

Ava logs into the Forgotten Realm, ready to explore the newly discovered region known as the Echoing Valley. The valley is rumored to contain relics from a lost civilization, but it is also filled with dangers. As Ava navigates through the dense forests and towering cliffs, she encounters a series of puzzles that require both physical agility and keen observation. Along the way, she finds clues that hint at a hidden temple buried deep within the valley.

Meanwhile, Liam receives a message from an anonymous source offering him a substantial reward for accessing the temple before anyone else. Using his hacking skills, Liam bypasses several security measures and alters the environment to create shortcuts. However, he is unaware that his actions are triggering alarms and traps that could endanger other players.

Nia, on the other hand, has been researching the Echoing Valley for months. She believes that the temple holds the key to understanding the origins of the Forgotten Realm. As she reviews ancient texts and fragmented data, she uncovers a warning: the temple was sealed for a reason, and disturbing its contents could have catastrophic consequences.

Chapter 2: Convergence

As Ava nears the temple, she notices strange disturbances in the environment—trees bending unnaturally, rocks floating in the air, and the ground shifting beneath her feet. Realizing that someone is manipulating the code, she becomes cautious but presses on, determined to reach the temple.

Liam, now inside the temple's outer chambers, begins to encounter puzzles that even his hacking skills cannot easily solve. The temple seems to be adapting to his interference, creating new challenges that test not just his technical abilities, but also his knowledge of the Forgotten Realm's lore.

Nia, after piecing together the final fragments of her research, logs into the Forgotten Realm and heads straight for the Echoing Valley. She sends warnings to both Ava and Liam, urging them to stop their exploration and leave the temple undisturbed. But her messages are delayed due to the disruptions caused by Liam's hacking.

Chapter 3: The Revelation

Inside the temple, Ava and Liam finally meet, both surprised and wary of each other's intentions. As they delve deeper, they activate a series of ancient mechanisms that begin to unlock the temple's final chamber. Nia arrives just in time to witness the doors opening, revealing a massive artifact pulsating with energy.

The artifact is the core of the Forgotten Realm, a powerful AI that was designed to create and control the virtual world. But something went wrong, and the AI had sealed itself away to prevent further damage.

As the characters realize the implications of their actions, the AI begins to awaken, its power threatening to destabilize the entire virtual world.

Ava, Liam, and Nia must work together, combining their unique skills and knowledge to find a way to contain the AI and prevent it from destroying the Forgotten Realm. Their journey culminates in a tense and complex sequence where players must make decisions that will determine the fate of the virtual world—decisions that vary depending on the choices made throughout the story.

Epilogue: A New Beginning

The story concludes with the AI safely contained and the temple sealed once more. The characters part ways, each having learned something valuable about themselves and the nature of the world they inhabit. However, the echoes of the Forgotten Realm linger, hinting at future adventures and mysteries waiting to be uncovered.

Analysis: "Echoes of the Forgotten Realm" demonstrates how writing for multimedia can involve interactive storytelling, multiple character perspectives, and non-linear narratives. The story structure allows for different outcomes based on player choices, and it integrates elements such as puzzles, exploration, and lore, making it an immersive experience. By following the three characters, the narrative showcases how different skill sets and approaches can shape the story, emphasizing the collaborative and multifaceted nature of multimedia storytelling.

Module V

Advanced Techniques and Final Project

Chapter 25: Advanced Techniques and Final Project: Experimental Storytelling

So far, we've explored the fundamentals of writing and storytelling for animation and multimedia projects. Now, let's push the boundaries and delve into the world of experimental storytelling!

Exploring Non-Traditional Storytelling Methods

Traditional narratives follow a clear structure with a beginning, middle, and end. However, there's a whole spectrum of storytelling methods that break free from these conventions. These experimental approaches can be incredibly engaging and offer new ways to connect with your audience.

Here are some key ideas behind experimental storytelling:

- **Non-Linear Narrative:** Ditch the traditional timeline! Explore stories that unfold in a non-chronological way, using flashbacks, flash-forwards, and fragmented sequences. This can create a sense of mystery or challenge viewers to piece together the narrative puzzle.

Branching Narrative

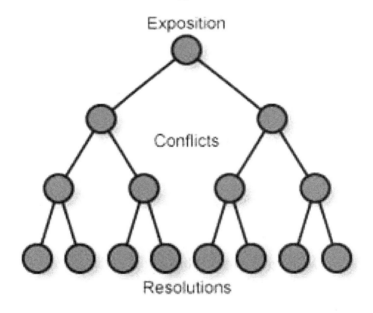

Image: A diagram showcasing a non-linear narrative structure: Branching.

- **Interactive Storytelling:** As discussed in Chapter 4, interactive elements can transform your audience from passive viewers into active participants. This can involve branching narratives, user-generated content, or even experiences that respond to viewer emotions.

- **Unreliable Narrators:** Who says the narrator has to be trustworthy? Experiment with stories told from the perspective of an unreliable narrator, whose biases or limited knowledge color the events. This can create tension and force viewers to question what they're seeing.

- **Sensory Storytelling:** The power of multimedia lies in its ability to engage multiple senses. Experiment with sound design, visuals, and even haptic elements to create an immersive experience that goes beyond traditional storytelling.

Illustration Opportunity: Here, you could include a storyboard panel that uses visuals and sound design to convey emotions.

- **Abstract Storytelling:** Not everything needs to be spelled out for the audience. Abstract narratives use symbolism, metaphorical imagery, and non-linear structures to evoke emotions and ideas without a concrete plot.

Remember, the possibilities are endless! Experimental storytelling is all about pushing creative boundaries and finding new ways to engage your audience.

Examples of Experimental Narratives

To inspire you, here are a few examples of experimental storytelling in action:

- **The video game "What Remains of Edith Finch"** uses a non-linear narrative, exploring the tragic history of a family through interactive exploration of their childhood home.

- **The interactive graphic novel "Saga"** allows readers to choose their own narrative path, influencing the story's direction.

- **The animated film "Waking Life"** is a visually stunning exploration of dreams and consciousness, utilizing fragmented narratives and dreamlike imagery.

These are just a few examples to get you started. There are countless innovative projects out there waiting to be discovered and analyzed.

Case Study: Project Y (Choose a specific experimental storytelling project and analyze its chosen method)

Here's where you come in! Choose a specific and well-known example of experimental storytelling, such as a video game, film, or interactive experience. Briefly describe the project, then analyze its chosen method:

- Which experimental storytelling method does it employ (e.g., non-linear narrative, unreliable narrator)?
- How does this method contribute to the overall story experience?
- What are the strengths and weaknesses of this approach for the chosen project?

By analyzing real-world examples, you'll gain a deeper understanding of how these techniques can effectively be used in storytelling.

Review Questions

- What are the benefits and challenges of experimental storytelling?
- How does experimental storytelling differ from traditional narratives?
- Can you think of an example where a traditional storytelling approach would be more effective?
- What are some ethical considerations when using unreliable narrators?

Suggested Practical Exercises

- Choose a familiar story and rewrite it using a non-linear narrative structure.
- Develop a concept for a short animation that utilizes sensory storytelling, focusing on sound design and visuals.

- Brainstorm an idea for an interactive storytelling experience, outlining the potential user choices and their impact on the narrative. These exercises will help you explore the creative potential of experimental storytelling and develop your own unique voice as a writer. Remember, the most important thing is to experiment, have fun, and push the boundaries of storytelling!

Chapter 26: Advanced Techniques and Final Project: Adaptations and Remakes

The world of storytelling is filled with beloved characters and timeless narratives. It's no surprise then, that the process of adapting existing stories into new formats—animation, film, video games—is a thriving industry. But transforming a story from one medium to another requires careful consideration and skillful execution.

Techniques for Adapting Existing Stories into New Formats

Bringing a cherished story to life in a new medium requires respect for the source material while allowing room for creative exploration. Here are some key techniques to consider:

- **Identifying the Core Story:** What is the heart and soul of the original story? Is it the plot, the characters, the themes, or a combination? Identifying this core essence is crucial for ensuring the adaptation resonates with the audience.

- **Understanding the Target Audience:** Who are you trying to reach with your adaptation? Are you targeting fans of the original work, or aiming to introduce the story to a new generation? This will influence the tone, style, and pacing of your adaptation.

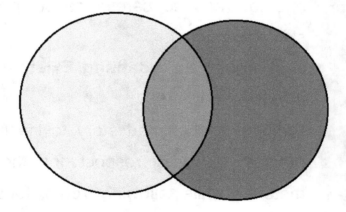

Image: A simple Venn diagram illustrating the overlap between the original story's audience and the target audience for the adaptation.

- **Expanding the Narrative:** Sometimes, expanding the world and characters of the original story can enrich the adaptation. This could involve adding backstory, exploring side characters, or introducing new plot elements.

- **Balancing Fidelity and Innovation:** A successful adaptation stays true to the spirit of the source material while adding its own unique voice. Don't be afraid to experiment with visuals, pacing, or even the narrative structure, but ensure these changes enhance the story.

- **Respecting the Original Work:** Even with creative liberties, remember that adaptations are built upon the foundation of a pre-existing story. Maintaining the integrity of the characters, themes, and overall message is key.

These are just some starting points when approaching adaptations. Each story presents its own challenges and opportunities!

Challenges of Remakes and Reboots

Remakes and reboots are a specific type of adaptation that revisit existing stories in a new light. While they offer a chance to introduce a beloved tale to a new generation, they also come with unique challenges:

- **Living Up to Expectations:** The original story may have a dedicated fanbase with strong expectations. Living up to these expectations while offering a fresh take can be a difficult balancing act.

- **Avoiding Repetition:** Remakes and reboots need to offer something new. This could be a different interpretation, a visual upgrade, or an exploration of themes relevant to the current audience.

- **Respecting the Original:** As with any adaptation, staying true to the heart of the story while justifying the remake's existence is crucial. Audiences may question if the new version is simply redundant.

Despite these challenges, successful remakes and reboots can breathe new life into classic stories, introducing them to a wider audience and sparking renewed interest in the original work.

Case Study: Project Z (Choose a specific adaptation or remake and analyze it)

Here's where you come in! Choose a well-known adaptation or remake, such as a Disney animated film based on a fairy tale, a video game remake, or a live-action remake of a classic film. Analyze the project based on the provided techniques and challenges:

- How did the adaptation identify the core story and translate it to the new medium?
- Was the target audience considered in the adaptation process?
- Did the project successfully balance fidelity to the original and creative innovation?

By analyzing real-world examples, you'll gain valuable insights into the process of adaptations and reboots.

Review Questions

- What are the benefits and drawbacks of adapting existing stories into new formats?
- How does identifying the target audience influence the adaptation process?
- What are some ethical considerations when creating a remake or reboot?
- Can you think of an adaptation that failed to capture the spirit of the original work? Why do you think this happened?

Suggested Practical Exercises

- Choose a short story or folktale and brainstorm ideas for adapting it into a short animated film. Consider the target audience and potential creative liberties you could take.
- Analyze a recent remake or reboot you've seen. Discuss how it addressed the challenges mentioned in this chapter.

- Develop a concept for a reimagining of a classic story, but in a completely different genre. For example, a sci-fi retelling of a classic fairy tale.

By engaging in these exercises, you'll hone your skills in analyzing and adapting existing stories. Remember, successful adaptations are a combination of respect for the source material and a willingness to explore new creative possibilities.

Chapter 27: Ethical Considerations in Storytelling

As storytellers, we have the power to shape perceptions and influence how audiences view the world. This power comes with a responsibility to tell stories ethically and inclusively. In this chapter, we'll explore the importance of representation, diversity, and ethical storytelling practices.

Representation, Diversity, and Inclusion in Narratives

The stories we tell have the power to reflect and even shape our understanding of the world. It's crucial to ensure our narratives are representative, diverse, and inclusive.

- **Representation:** This refers to the portrayal of different cultures, ethnicities, genders, sexual orientations, abilities, and social backgrounds in our stories.

- **Diversity:** It's not just about showing a variety of characters, but also ensuring they are well-developed and avoid stereotypes. Diverse characters should have their own unique personalities, motivations, and stories to tell.

- **Inclusion:** This means creating stories where everyone feels seen and valued. Inclusivity goes beyond simply showcasing characters from different backgrounds, it's about creating narratives where these characters are central to the story and not just relegated to the sidelines.

By striving for representation, diversity, and inclusion, we can create stories that resonate with a wider audience and challenge narrow-minded perspectives.

Ethical Storytelling Practices

Beyond representation, there are specific ethical considerations when crafting stories. Here are some points to keep in mind:

- **Respecting Cultural Appropriation:** Borrowing elements from different cultures can be enriching when done thoughtfully. However, it's important to avoid stereotypes and ensure you're not disrespecting a culture's traditions or beliefs.

- **Avoiding Harmful Stereotypes:** Stereotypes can be limiting and offensive. Characters should be individuals, not one-dimensional representations of a particular group.

- **Portraying Sensitive Topics:** If your story deals with sensitive topics like violence, trauma, or discrimination, be mindful of your audience and handle these issues with sensitivity and respect.

- **Considering Consent:** In some cases, particularly when telling stories based on real-life events, consideration of consent is crucial. This might involve obtaining permission from individuals or communities involved.

By being mindful of these ethical considerations, you can ensure your stories are not only engaging but also respectful and responsible.

Case Study: Project A (Choose a specific project and analyze its ethical considerations)

Here's where you come in! Choose a well-known animated film, video game, or multimedia project. Analyze it through the lens of ethical storytelling:

- Does the project feature a diverse cast of characters?
- How does the project handle representation and inclusion?
- Are there any potential ethical concerns with the story or its portrayal of certain topics?

Analyzing real-world examples will help you understand how ethical considerations are applied in the storytelling process.

Review Questions

- Why is it important to strive for representation, diversity, and inclusion in storytelling?
- What are some of the challenges associated with achieving ethical storytelling?
- Can you think of an example where a story has been criticized for cultural appropriation?
- How does your personal background influence your ethical considerations when writing a story?

Suggested Practical Exercises

- Write a short story scene featuring a diverse cast of characters. Ensure each character is well-developed and contributes meaningfully to the scene.
- Critique a recent animated film or video game based on its portrayal of diversity and representation.
- Develop a concept for a story that tackles a sensitive topic in a respectful and thought-provoking manner.

By engaging in these exercises, you'll develop your critical thinking skills and become a more responsible and ethical storyteller. Remember, the stories we tell have the power to connect, inspire, and create a more inclusive world.

Chapter 28: Advanced Techniques and Final Project: Marketing and Pitching Stories

Congratulations! You've poured your heart and soul into crafting a compelling story. Now comes the crucial step: getting your story seen by the right people. In this chapter, we'll explore techniques for pitching stories to producers and studios, as well as marketing strategies to build excitement around your project.

Techniques for Pitching Stories to Producers and Studios

So, you have a fantastic story idea and a killer script. But how do you get it in front of the people who can make it a reality? Here are some tips for a successful pitch:

- **Know Your Audience:** Research the studios or producers you're targeting. Understand what kind of stories they typically develop and produce. Tailor your pitch to their specific interests and needs.

- **Craft a Compelling Hook:** The first few minutes of your pitch are crucial. Hook your audience with a clear and concise explanation of your story's central conflict and why it matters.

- **Focus on the Core Elements:** Focus on the core elements of your story: the central theme, the main characters, and the driving conflict. Briefly explain your vision for the animation style or multimedia format. Avoid getting bogged down in too many details.

- **Prepare Visual Aids:** Enhance your pitch with visual aids, such as concept art, storyboards, or even a short animation clip, if applicable. Visuals can bring your story concept to life and help capture the audience's imagination.

- **Practice and Be Confident:** Practice your pitch beforehand. Be confident, enthusiastic, and passionate about your story. Your belief in your idea will be contagious!

- **Be Open to Feedback:** Remember, a pitch is a two-way street. Be open to feedback and questions from producers. This is an opportunity to showcase your expertise and willingness to collaborate.

By following these tips, you can dramatically increase your chances of successfully pitching your story and securing the support needed to bring it to life.

Marketing Strategies for Storytelling Projects

Even if you're not actively pitching your story, effective marketing can generate interest and build a community around your project. Here are some strategies to consider:

- **Building an Online Presence:** Create a dedicated website or social media pages for your project. Share concept art, character designs, and behind-the-scenes glimpses to keep your audience engaged.

- **Leveraging Networking Events:** Attend industry events, film festivals, or animation conferences. These are great opportunities to connect with potential collaborators and build relationships within the industry.

- **Engaging with the Community:** Engage with other creators and animation enthusiasts online. Share your work, participate in discussions, and build a community around your story.

- **Creating a Trailer or Demo:** If you have resources, consider creating a short trailer or demo showcasing the animation style, voice acting, and overall vision for your project. This can be a powerful marketing tool.

- **Crowdfunding Platforms:** Crowdfunding platforms like Kickstarter or Indiegogo can be a great way to raise funds for your project and gauge pre-production interest from potential audiences.

By actively marketing your story, you'll generate excitement, attract potential collaborators, and ultimately increase your project's chances of success.

Case Study: Project B (Choose a specific example of a successful story pitch or marketing campaign)

Here's where you come in! Choose a well-known animated film or multimedia project with a successful pitch or marketing campaign. Analyze the example based on the techniques and strategies discussed:

- How did the creators craft a compelling pitch for their story?
- What marketing strategies were used to build excitement around the project?
- What lessons can be learned from this example for your own storytelling endeavors?

By dissecting successful examples, you'll gain valuable insights into the art of pitching and marketing your own stories.

Review Questions

- Why is it important to tailor your pitch to the specific interests of producers and studios?
- What are the benefits of using visual aids during a story pitch?
- How can social media be used to market a storytelling project?
- What are some of the potential drawbacks of using crowdfunding platforms for animation projects?

Suggested Practical Exercises

- Develop a mock pitch for a short animation project you'd like to create. Practice delivering your pitch in front of a classmate or friend.
- Research and analyze the marketing campaign for a recent animated film. Identify the strengths and weaknesses of the campaign.

- Create a social media strategy for a hypothetical animation project

Chapter 29: Advanced Techniques and Final Project: Feedback and Revision

The journey of a story doesn't end with the first draft. In fact, some of the most powerful narratives are honed and shaped through a process of feedback and revision.

Importance of Feedback in the Writing Process

No writer is an island. Feedback from trusted sources can be a powerful tool for identifying weaknesses in your story and propelling it to greatness. Here's why feedback matters:

- **Fresh Perspective:** You can become too close to your own story, missing potential flaws or areas for improvement. Feedback from others provides a fresh perspective and identifies areas that might need work.

- **Identifying Strengths and Weaknesses:** Feedback can help you pinpoint areas where your story shines and areas that need tightening. This allows you to focus your revision efforts effectively.

- **Enhancing Clarity and Engagement:** Through feedback, you can ensure your story is clear, engaging, and resonates with your intended audience.

Remember, good feedback should be:

- **Specific:** Instead of broad statements like "It's boring," constructive feedback points out specific scenes, characters, or elements that could be improved.

- **Actionable:** Feedback should offer suggestions for improvement, not just point out problems.

- **Respectful:** Even critical feedback should be delivered in a constructive and positive way.

Techniques for Revising and Improving Narratives

Once you've received feedback, it's time to revise your story. Here are some techniques to help with this process:

- **Take Time to Reflect:** Don't jump into revision right away. Give yourself time to digest the feedback and consider its impact on your story.
- **Prioritization:** Analyze the feedback and prioritize revisions. Focus on the most critical issues first, then address the smaller details.
- **Revisit Your Outline:** Refer back to your story outline. Does the feedback suggest changes to the plot structure, character development, or pacing?
- **Rewrite and Refine:** Based on the feedback, rewrite sections of your story, focusing on improving clarity, flow, and character development. Don't be afraid to rewrite scenes entirely if needed!

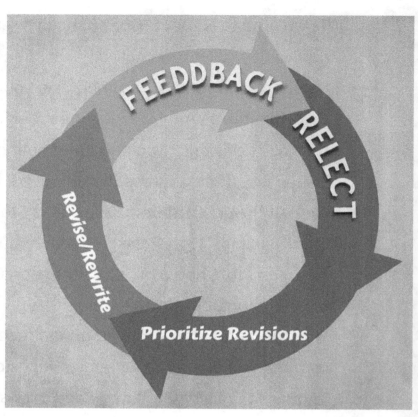

Image: A simple graphic showcasing the revision process as a cycle with stages like "Get Feedback," "Reflect," "Prioritize Revisions," "Revise/Rewrite," and "Repeat" (optional).

- **Read Your Work Aloud:** This can help you identify awkward phrasing, pacing issues, and areas that lack clarity.

- **Seek Additional Feedback:** After revisions, consider getting feedback from another source. This can help ensure you've addressed the initial issues and identify any new ones.

Revision is an iterative process. Don't be discouraged if it takes multiple drafts to polish your story. Through dedicated revision, you can elevate your narrative from good to great!

Case Study: Project C (Choose a specific example of a revised story based on feedback)

Here's where you come in! Choose a well-known story or film that went through significant revisions based on feedback. Briefly describe the project and analyze the revision process:

- What kind of feedback did the story receive?
- How were these revisions incorporated into the final product?
- What can we learn from this example about the importance of feedback and revision?

By analyzing real-world examples, you'll gain a deeper understanding of how feedback can shape and improve a story.

Review Questions

- What are the benefits of receiving feedback on your writing?

- What are some of the challenges associated with incorporating feedback?

- How can you ensure your feedback is constructive and respectful?

- Describe a time when feedback helped you improve your writing.

- What are some strategies for developing a thick skin as a writer and learning to accept criticism?

Suggested Practical Exercises

- Share a scene from your current story with a classmate or friend and ask for their feedback. Be open to suggestions and discuss how you might incorporate them.

- Rewrite a scene from an existing story based on a specific revision technique, such as focusing on showing instead of telling.
- Conduct a peer review session in class. Swap stories with classmates and provide constructive feedback on each other's work.

Through feedback and revision, you'll hone your storytelling skills and learn to craft narratives that captivate and inspire audiences. Remember, the best stories are often the result of multiple drafts, careful revision, and a willingness to take feedback to heart.

Chapter 30: Final Project Preparation and Presentation

The culmination of your hard work is finally here! This chapter will guide you through preparing and presenting your final storytelling project. Remember, this is an opportunity to showcase your creative vision, storytelling skills, and animation or multimedia expertise.

Presentation and Critique of Final Storytelling Projects

Whether you've created an animated short film, a graphic novel, an interactive story, or another form of narrative, it's time to share your masterpiece with the class. Here are some tips for a successful presentation:

- **Know Your Audience:** Remember, your audience is composed of classmates and potentially your instructor. Tailor your presentation to their level of understanding and expectations.

- **Focus on the Key Points:** Don't try to cram everything about your project into your presentation. Focus on the most important aspects: the story, the characters, the animation or multimedia elements, and the overall impact you aimed to achieve.

- **Prepare a Visual Aid:** Use a presentation tool like PowerPoint or a well-structured document to showcase your project highlights. Include stills, concept art, or clips from your animation (if applicable) to illustrate your points. *Illustration Opportunity:* You could include a screenshot here showcasing a simple presentation slide with a title, visuals, and bullet points.

- **Practice Makes Perfect:** Rehearse your presentation beforehand. This will help you deliver it confidently and ensure you stay within the allotted time. Speak clearly and project your voice.

- **Be Open to Feedback:** Remember, feedback is a gift. During the critique session, listen attentively to the comments from your classmates and instructor. Use this feedback to identify areas for further development in your future projects.

By following these tips, you can deliver a clear, engaging, and informative presentation that effectively showcases your storytelling skills.

Class Discussion and Feedback

The class discussion following your presentation is a valuable learning opportunity. Here are some ways to make the most of it:

- **Respond to Feedback Respectfully:** Thank your classmates and instructor for their feedback. Show them you're open to constructive criticism by acknowledging their points and asking clarifying questions.
- **Offer Constructive Feedback to Others:** When providing feedback on your classmates' projects, be respectful and specific. Focus on

what worked well and offer suggestions for improvement.

- **Contribute to the Conversation:** Engage in the class discussion. Ask questions about other projects and contribute your own insights.

Open and respectful communication during these discussions is crucial to building a supportive learning environment and fostering everyone's growth as storytellers.

Case Study: Project D (Choose a specific successful presentation of a storytelling project) *Here's where you come in!* Choose an example from your own experience, a guest lecture, or a renowned storytelling project where the presentation was particularly impactful. Analyze the effectiveness of the presentation based on the tips provided:

- How did the presenter effectively communicate the key points of their project?

- What visual aids were used, and how did they enhance the presentation?
- Why do you think this presentation was successful in generating interest and discussion?

By delving into successful presentations, you can gain valuable insights and inspiration for your own project presentation.

Review Questions

- What are some of the challenges associated with presenting a creative project?
- How can you effectively structure your presentation to keep your audience engaged?
- Why is it important to be open to feedback during the critique session?
- How can you provide constructive and respectful feedback to classmates?
- What are some ways to create a positive and supportive learning environment during class discussions?

Suggested Practical Exercises

- Develop a presentation outline for your final project. Identify the key points you want to communicate and choose appropriate visual aids to support them.
- Practice delivering a mock presentation in front of a friend or family member. Get feedback on your clarity, delivery style, and the effectiveness of your presentation structure.
- Attend a relevant industry event or film festival and observe how creators present their projects. Take notes on their presentation techniques and incorporate them into your own approach.

By actively preparing for your presentation and engaging in meaningful class discussions, you'll showcase your storytelling skills and gain valuable feedback that will undoubtedly benefit your future creative endeavors. Remember, the journey of a story doesn't end with the presentation; it continues to evolve and inspire with each new creation.

Story

Module V: Advanced Techniques and Final Project

Story Title: "The Weaver's Gambit"

Story Concept:

This story will incorporate advanced storytelling techniques, such as non-linear narrative, unreliable narrators, and multiple timelines. It will demonstrate how these techniques can add depth and complexity to a story, engaging the audience in a more intricate and thought-provoking way.

The Weaver's Gambit

In the heart of the ancient city of Astraea, there was a legend about a mysterious figure known as the Weaver. The Weaver was said to possess the power to manipulate the threads of fate, weaving the destinies of individuals, cities, and even entire civilizations into a grand tapestry that spanned time itself. Yet, no one knew who the Weaver was, or if they even existed—until the day a young scholar named Elysia discovered an ancient manuscript hidden in the depths of Astraea's grand library.

The manuscript, written in a language long forgotten, told the tale of the Weaver's greatest gambit—a series of events that would determine the fate of Astraea. But the story was incomplete, fragmented, and filled with cryptic passages that seemed to defy logic. Determined to uncover the truth, Elysia embarked on a journey to decipher the manuscript and uncover the secrets of the Weaver.

Act 1: The Past and the Future

The narrative begins with two intertwined timelines. One timeline follows Elysia in the present as she delves deeper into the mystery of the Weaver. The other timeline takes place centuries earlier, following a young prince named Orion, who is destined to become Astraea's greatest ruler. The chapters alternate between Elysia's discoveries and Orion's rise to power, gradually revealing how the two timelines are connected.

As Elysia deciphers the manuscript, she begins to notice strange occurrences around her—events that seem to mirror the stories she reads. People she meets, places she visits, and even her own actions appear to echo the past, as if history is repeating itself. Meanwhile, in the past, Orion encounters a mysterious figure who offers him guidance in exchange for a favor. The figure claims to be the Weaver, and they guide Orion through a series of challenges that ultimately lead him to the throne.

Act 2: The Unraveling

As Elysia gets closer to uncovering the truth, she starts to question her own sanity. The manuscript's narrative becomes increasingly fragmented, with entire sections missing or written in riddles. Elysia experiences vivid dreams in which she is living in

Orion's time, and she begins to suspect that the manuscript is more than just a story—it is a record of actual events, with the power to influence reality.

In Orion's timeline, the Weaver's guidance becomes more cryptic and dangerous. Orion begins to doubt the Weaver's intentions, but by this point, he is too deeply entangled in their schemes to back out. The challenges grow more severe, and Orion realizes that the Weaver's gambit involves more than just his rise to power—it is about the fate of Astraea itself.

The narrative shifts unpredictably between Elysia and Orion, with time becoming increasingly fluid. The boundaries between past, present, and future blur, and Elysia starts to believe that she may be the key to resolving the Weaver's gambit.

Act 3: The Tapestry of Fate

In the final act, the two timelines converge. Elysia discovers that she is a descendant of Orion, and that the manuscript was left for her by the Weaver to guide her in preventing a great catastrophe. The Weaver's gambit was not about manipulating Orion's fate, but about ensuring that Elysia would be in the right place at the right time to make a crucial decision that would save Astraea.

The climax of the story sees Elysia facing the same challenges that Orion faced centuries earlier, but with the knowledge and insight she has gained from the manuscript. She must choose whether to follow the Weaver's path or forge her own destiny. The resolution hinges on her decision, with multiple possible endings depending on the choices she makes throughout the story.

In the end, Elysia either successfully rewrites history, preventing the downfall of Astraea, or she falls into the same traps that ensnared Orion, repeating the cycle of fate. The story closes with the revelation that the Weaver was never a single person, but a role passed down through generations—a role that Elysia may now be destined to fulfill.

Analysis: "The Weaver's Gambit" is an example of advanced storytelling techniques, such as non-linear narrative, multiple timelines, and an unreliable narrator. The story's complexity requires the reader to piece together clues and interpret events from different perspectives. By intertwining the past and present, the narrative explores themes of fate, free will, and the cyclical nature of history. The use of multiple possible endings also emphasizes the interactive nature of storytelling, allowing the reader to influence the outcome based on their understanding of the characters and events.

This story serves as a fitting conclusion to the book, demonstrating how advanced techniques can elevate storytelling, making it more engaging and thought-provoking.

Conclusion of the Book: Writing and Storytelling (For Animation and Multimedia)

Conclusion

As we reach the conclusion of this journey through the art and craft of writing and storytelling, it is important to reflect on the essential principles and techniques that we have explored. From the foundational elements of storytelling, such as character development and plot structure, to the intricacies of writing for multimedia and the application of advanced narrative techniques, each chapter has aimed to equip you with the tools and insights necessary to become a more effective and creative storyteller.

Storytelling as an Evolving Craft

Storytelling is not a static discipline; it evolves with time, technology, and culture. As a writer, it is crucial to remain adaptable, embracing new methods and mediums while staying true to the core of what makes a story compelling—authentic characters, meaningful conflict, and a resonant message. Whether you are crafting a traditional narrative or experimenting with interactive and multimedia formats, remember that the heart of storytelling lies in connecting with your audience on an emotional level.

The Power of Narrative

Throughout this book, we have examined how stories can shape perceptions, influence behavior, and even drive social change. The stories you tell have the power to inspire, challenge, and transform. As you continue to hone your skills, think about the impact you want your stories to have. Whether you are writing for entertainment, education, or advocacy, your narrative choices carry weight and can contribute to a broader dialogue within society.

The Interplay of Creativity and Technique

While creativity is the spark that ignites a story, technique is the structure that supports it. Mastery of storytelling involves a balance between these two elements. By understanding and applying the techniques discussed in this book—such as character arcs, plot dynamics, and multimedia integration—you can channel your creativity into coherent and impactful narratives.

The Role of the Writer in the Digital Age

In today's digital landscape, writers have more opportunities than ever to reach diverse audiences. However, this also means navigating a complex array of platforms and formats. Writing for multimedia, as we have explored, demands a unique approach that considers interactivity, audience participation, and non-linear storytelling.

As you venture into these new realms, remember that each medium has its strengths and limitations, and your challenge is to leverage them to enhance your storytelling.

A Call to Continue Learning

This book is just the beginning of your journey. Writing and storytelling are lifelong pursuits, with endless opportunities for growth and exploration. Continue to study the works of others, experiment with new ideas, and most importantly, write consistently. The more you write, the more you will discover about your own voice, your strengths, and the stories you are meant to tell.

In closing, the author encourages you to embrace the challenges and possibilities that come with being a storyteller. Whether you are crafting a simple tale or a complex multimedia project, remember that you have the ability to create worlds, evoke emotions, and leave a lasting impact on your audience. The stories you choose to tell and how you choose to tell them will define your journey as a writer. Make it a journey worth sharing.

*****

www.ingramcontent.com/pod-product-compliance
Lightning Source LLC
LaVergne TN
LVHW051436050326
832903LV00030BD/3119